Qui-qui-ri-quí!

Cock of the Walk

Qui-qui-ri-qui!

The Legend of
PANCHO VILLA

By Haldeen Braddy

KENNIKAT PRESS
Port Washington, N. Y./London

Qui-qui-ri-qui!

COCK OF THE WALK

Copyright 1955 by Haldeen Braddy
Reissued in 1970 by Kennikat Press by arrangement
Library of Congress Catalog Card No: 79-85988
SBN 8046-0875-X

Manufactured by Taylor Publishing Company   Dallas, Texas

To My Mother

LENA ROUNDTREE BRADDY HARTSOOK

Preface

Pancho Villa has dominated my literary interest from the year 1935, when I moved from New York to Alpine, Texas. In Alpine, El Paso, Presidio, and other Texas-Mexico border towns I heard so many stirring tales about him that I visited shortly, in that same year, a few cities in Mexico, such as Chihuahua, Juárez, and Ojinaga. Again, in 1939, I traveled through the same border country. Much later, at El Paso in 1946 and thereafter, I interviewed people and visited battle scenes in Arizona, New Mexico, and Texas, and traveled in the interior of Mexico to Mexico City itself, visiting such other famous historical sites as Parral and Torreón.

My study of Villa, often interrupted by other duties, has comprised about twenty years of work, for the career of this *hombre* of the hills always has been somewhere near the forefront of my mind. It took me a long time to write *Cock of the Walk,* because it underwent many revisions, and, of course, a much longer time to gather all the materials which are in it. Throughout these labors, it has been my ambition to write a book that will report the true Villa once and for all.

One of my main objectives has been to tell the story of Villa from beginning to end. My book thus differs sharply from shorter books that report mainly on the Columbus Raid or, say, his relations with General Pershing, and equally sharply from movie versions that treat mainly of his lost treasures, or his imaginary return to Mexico as a deliverer. *Cock of the Walk* attempts to give adequate and proportional treatment to all phases of his career. I have sought to write not an episode or a series of incidents, as I did in my four or five published articles, but a full and well-rounded picture of the man.

Another of my objectives has been to present Villa as impartially as possible. It has been difficult to run a true course at all times, for many of the stories I have heard strikingly contradict each other. I have been obliged to act as a judge, to accept some reports and to reject others.

Villa made many enemies during his lifetime and was hard on foreigners living in his country. The Honorable Wellinton Chew, now a prominent lawyer in El Paso, was expelled from Mexico as a child during Villa's persecution of the Chinese. Mrs. Alfred Jean Abel, now a well-known El Pasoan, was descended from the famous Italian family of the Visconti. As a little girl, she saw her father killed and his properties confiscated. On the other hand, a number of Americans had reason to like Villa. This group included General Scott and members of his staff as well as his one-time foreman, Jimmie Caldwell, now of Santa Fe, New Mexico. Still a third group, Americans again, viewed him without strong bias as a natural, if fierce, leader of the Revolution. These men include Messrs. George A. Brown, a retired United States Deputy Marshal, and Chester Chope, of the El Paso *Herald-Post*. To these personages and others, such as Charles Leland Sonnichsen, who led me to one story of gold and another of ghosts, I am much indebted. In the bibliography I have endeavored to record yet other, more specific, obligations. I owe special thanks for help with revising the manuscript to my friend and colleague, Joseph Leach.

In my final appraisal, I have seen fit to pronounce Pancho Villa more cocky than bloodthirsty. The gorier escapades of that epoch were due to his hirelings, to Martin López or to Rodolfo Fierro, whom the famous author, Ambrose Bierce, referred to in his letters as El Matador Fierro. Thus I have not dwelled on some of the racier stories about Villa's treatment of Mrs. Wright and other ladies prior to and during the dark hour of his invasion of United States territory at Columbus, New Mexico. Though I should not wish to defend the cruel bandit that Villa finally became, I must confess that he was *mucho hombre,* that he was thoroughly masculine in loving the race track and cock fighting and at least understandable as a man in his virile passion for women. At his best, Pancho Villa was a peerless gamecock, crowing, to be sure, but always ready for a fight. Perhaps that is what he really was and what history will finally rate him.

HALDEEN BRADDY

Paso del Norte, April 25, 1955

PREFACE
TO THE SECOND EDITION

In the folklore of the Mexican Revolution of 1910-1920 Francisco "Pancho" Villa (1878-1923) remains today the central figure. This thesis of *Cock of the Walk* each year gains in acceptability. Other figures of that civil war — Madero, Carranza, Obregón, Calles — have half-faded into the history of half a century ago. The name of Villa, in contrast, shines among the Mexican people and among varied groups in a host of other nations. Folklore about the Man of a Million Faces is still active; the legend is still growing; with the result that his image today has become an imposing factor in modern Mexican history.

The stature of Villa as a crucial figure in the story of Mexican politics had developed in fifty years to the point that the congress of that country recently conferred upon him a special title. In November, 1966, Francisco Villa became "Hero of the Revolution" by vote of the national assembly of Mexico. This event followed by precisely fifty years the last drive of the resurgent Villa against the federal government headed by Venustiano Carranza, who suffered assassination a few months later. Bespectacled Carranza, a cultured man twice president of revolutionary Mexico and

x

dramatically killed while in office, is now remembered chiefly by scholars. Carranza's dedicated enemy, Villa, never came closer to public office than to pose sitting in the Mexican presidential chair; yet the name of Villa as a crude, unlettered adversary continues to be a household word within the borders of the Mexican Republic — and far beyond.

The colorful subject of rebellious Villa has naturally appealed strongly to biographers Mexican and otherwise. Native works of significance range from the rather scholarly annals by Martin Luis Guzmán y Franco to the sentimental recollections of the official widow, Luz Corral. Guzmán wrote *Memorias de Pancho Villa* (4 vols.) *El Aguila y la serpiente* (1938-1940); Doña Luz, *Pancho Villa en la intimidad* (1948). Among the more general treatments, Nellie Campbello's *Apuntes sobre la vida militar de Francisco Villa* (1940) ranks as an impartial historical work worth study; *Francisco Villa ante la historia* (1939), by Celia Herrera Enriquez, does not live up to the promise of its title as an historical judgment, showing anti-Villa bias. The Herrera Enriquez tome long has appealed to the enemies of Villa as a forceful statement of their point of view.

Among widely read foreign books, there are two by French authors: Pere Felix's *Pancho Villa,* which by 1960 had gone into its fifth Mexican edition; and Jean Camp's *En selle avec Pancho Villa,* a French source published in Spanish translation at Mexico City as *Cabalgando con Pancho Villa* (1956).

American writers, more predictably, have devoted pages and ink to that elusive personage in modern Mexican politics. One of the very best eye-witness accounts of those troubled times, Dr. I. Thord-Gray's *Gringo Rebel* (1960) contains illuminating sidelights on Villa which testify as to both his heroism and dedication. William D. Lansford published a full-length biography, called simply *Pancho Villa,* in 1965. Dr. Carlos E. Husk, who had met and had dealt with his subject, never published the seven-page manuscript on the career of Villa, which he wrote from fresh recollection in 1914; but fortunately I was able to secure official permission to print this document in *Western Review* (I, 50-53) in 1964. Col. C. C. Clendenen's awarded study, *The United States and Pancho Villa* (1961), logically touches on the rebel's life, although primarily a diplomatic history. So do Richard O'Connor's *Black Jack Pershing* (1961) and Leon Wolff's article in an *American Heritage* volume (1962) on the Punitive Expedition. Collaterally, Virginia Taylor has rendered into English (1965) the classic *Memorias* of Guzmán.

British devotees of the study of Villa include a London writer whom I first met in my office in El Paso. I refer to Ronald Atkin, who came from London to Mexico and then to El Paso in 1965 to finish gathering material for his project, *The Red Earth of Mexico.* In making this on-the-ground survey, the English visitor was afforded the hearty cooperation and financial support of the Mexican government. *Red Earth,* says its author, will serve as a history of the modern Mexican Revolution, with a focus on Villa. The following year I repaid the Atkins visit to El Paso, as a guest of the officers of the Westerners Club in London, which has manifested a specific and objective interest in Pancho Villa. In June, 1967, I addressed the London chapter of the Westerners, meeting there Joseph G. Rosa, Colin Rickards, and others of the membership.

Besides the present volume, I have produced over a period of some twenty years a dozen articles about Villa, a book-length review of the Punitive Expedition, and one thirty-six page anthology based on several previous pieces: by title *Pancho Villa Rides Again,* published by Dr. S. D. Myres at his Paisano Press in 1967. The articles have ranged the gamut: the protean nature of Villa; his stature as folk hero; his accomplishments, his weaknesses, and his excesses; his relations with women; and his fabled gold. The first in this series appeared in the *New Mexico Folklore Review* for 1950-51: "Dorotello Arango, alias Pancho Villa." The latest, "Mexican Revolutionaries of 1910," appeared in the October, 1969 issue of *Montana, the Magazine of Western History.* There is much more interest in Villa today than when *Cock of the Walk* was first printed in 1955. This, I think, is homage he deserves; and I am now inclined to let it stand at that.

The University of Texas at El Paso,   H.B.
November, 1969

Contents

Qui-qui-ri-quí!

The Great River

The Rio Grande del Norte, beginning in Colorado and running through New Mexico, flows thinly into El Paso, where it divides the twin cities of the border—El Paso, Texas, and Ciudad Juárez, Chihuahua—and then heads south. At one point only, in Santa Elena Canyon, the river roars in a mighty torrent; everywhere else it is meek, modulated, shallow, and slow. Before reaching Del Rio, the Great River of the North has described a tremendous arc; some four hundred miles of meandered territory. But at Del Rio the waters of the Pecos are added; and now the Great River, picking up momentum, flows toward Brownsville and the Gulf of Mexico. Behind, back in the Big Bend country, the channel is narrow, the water sluggish; for here the Great River mocks the grandeur of its name. Neither broad nor deep, the Rio at El Paso has, on north and south sides, hundreds of miles of arid country. Trickling like a creek, it cuts through the silence and stillness of the desert land, barren, waterless, dead.

Here, on the southern side, in the states of Chihuahua, Coahuila, Durango, and Sonora, a man broke the placid tenor of the land of *mañana,* interrupted the *siestas* of *señores y señoritas* resting in the shade, and gave this des-

ert the electric pulse of vibrant life. The river, from its
source high in the untracked mountains of Colorado
throughout its descent to Santa Elena Canyon and on beyond to the sea, followed in its course the life of notorious Pancho Villa. In a convergence of the twain, the
history of this *hombre* during the Revolution of 1910-
1914 matched the turbulent stages of the river's course.
Once, and once only, in Santa Elena Canyon, does the
Rio roar in its awful majesty. Once, and once only, in the
legendary days of Villa, did the sleeping border awake
violently to the noise of his blood-curdling *gritos* with
which he rallied his forces, and the thunder of their
hoofbeats bent on revenge.

Along the banks of the Rio Grande and in the desert
states of northwest Mexico, people tell tales of the *bandido* Pancho Villa and of the adventurous men who
fought with him. In quick sequence, Villa changed
from *peon* to criminal, from criminal to avenger, from
avenger to lover, from lover to bandit, from bandit to
general, and finally from general to beloved champion
of the folk. Afterwards, at Villa's zenith as a fighting
rebel, his men and his *soldaderas,* the enthusiastic women
who followed them to battle, sang loud, rough songs like
this *corrido.*

> On the twenty-third of June, 1916,
> I address those who are present,
> Pancho Villa stormed the city,
> Taking it by front and rear.
>
> All the streets of Zacatecas
> Were piled high with slain Federalists,
> And the few who were not slaughtered
> Early in the day had fled.

For some Federals were so frightened
That they hid in women's skirts,
Pulling them up over trousers
And *mantillas* over blouses.

Somehow, out of slavery and imprisonment, in revolution and retirement, after war and peace, through disgrace and honor, Villa has emerged into a full-scaled myth. He wore many faces, this *hombre* who was both traitor and patriot, both a scoundrel and a friend of children. The downfall of betrayers and a loyal leader of the faithful, he was yet, above all, a lusty, bawdy, singing lover. One of the favorite songs he sang, *"La Cucaracha,"* or "The Cockroach," always ended with a refrain of longing.

Para sarapes, Saltillo;
Chihuahua para soldados;
Para mujeres, Jalisco;
Para el amor, toditos lados!

For serapes, Saltillo;
For soldiers, Chihuahua;
For women, Jalisco;
For love, everywhere!

The *cuentos,* or folktales, told about Villa in Mexico and in the Southwest along the borders of Arizona, New Mexico, and Texas may arise from the circumstance that legends develop best on far-flung frontiers of civilization in an epic age—when, among the people, there still lives a faith in the heroic, if not in the miraculous itself. When the peasants suffered under the weary load of feudalistic oppression, their imaginative impulses found release in thoughts of a messiah who would rise to their defense. The *peones,* the common people of Mexico, sought and found in Pancho Villa a deliverer who wreaked vengeance upon their despotic overlords. Pancho possessed the qualities of the heroic because so many of his deeds reveal his own folk background as well as the interests of his downtrodden, suppressed class. He became the scourge of evildoers and oppressors. Like an epic champion, he became the performer of daredevil stunts and well-nigh superhuman exploits.

A parallel has always been drawn between Pancho Villa and Robin Hood, sometimes with an actual basis in the facts of history, for a number of the seemingly tall stories told of him staunchly uphold the comparison.

Robin Hood, who, in 1160, was born the noble Robert Fitzooth of Locksley, lived with his yeomen in Sherwood Forest, near the famous river Trent, in Nottinghamshire. He befriended women and children, often sharing the spoils he stole from rich clergymen and wealthy knights with widows and orphans or with whoever was needy. The outlaws lived in the wood, on supplies robbed from travelers and on the king's deer which they shot. Robin had a celebrated longbow and, in story, a golden arrow. His chronicle reports that he was bled to death by one of his own caste, in the year 1247.

Now, Pancho Villa had a different name at birth, too, and he and his men likewise frequented the wild hills of the Sierra Madre, far to the south of the Rio Grande. Pancho, a sentimental outlaw, waxed most stern and cruel when he dealt with greedy priests or rich cattle barons. To match Robin's longbow, legend gave him a remarkable sword, on whose blade a curious motto was said to be carved: "A sure cure for any disease." At his end he was betrayed, not by the nobility he detested, but by one of the peasants for whom he had struggled. His ballad developed into a melodramatic version of the medieval original. But at the outset he was no tougher than his English progenitor, who himself often did more than poach on the deer of his overlord. The English folk hero stole from the churches, murdered noblemen, and frightened many a fair and virtuous lady nearly out of her wits.

Thus there existed a kinship between the two, rough as the defender of the *peones* became. The English robber hated the law and its agent, the Sheriff of Nottingham; Villa despised the feudal rule and its representative despot, Don Luis Terrazas. Like the gay denizen of Sherwood Forest, he robbed the churches, hounded the rich, but fought for the poor, gave them alms, and blessed their children. The simple country peasants loved him for his kindness and composed *corridos* about his adventures, which they sang at *bailes* and around campfires in Revolutionary days.

In fact, a main element of the medieval saga carried over into Villa's personal life. The singer, Ochoa, was his Alan-a-Dale; Trillo, the trusted right-hand man, his Little John; and Señora María Luz Corral, his Maid Marian. What the river Trent was to Robin Hood, the fabled Rio Grande was to Pancho Villa. It is small wonder, after all these years, that the older *peones* still sometimes leave burning candles in their windows at night to guide this magnificent Mexican, his trusted *segundo,* Trillo, and all his wild-riding men to a final, victorious Revolution.

Pancho Villa, even in the eyes of non-partisans, was certainly picturesque. None but the coldest heart could

fail to pulse with excitement when told of the mad rides
he used to make on glorious moonlit nights, during the
Revolution, to assemble his impromptu army of followers. As he rode through a settlement, the door of a house
suddenly would be pierced by a quivering blade flashing
in the moonlight. The dagger was an invitation to
join Villa's band; the smart *hombre* hastened outside,
grabbed the knife, and galloped quickly away with these
unrestrained, unpredictable rebels into adventures filled
with bloodshed and laughter. Whenever Villa captured
a town, he soon determined who was for or against him.
He banged on the door, shouting, *"Quien vive?"* The
only sensible reply was to answer with his vibrant rallying cry, *"Viva Villa! Viva Villa!"* For years this
bandido and revolutionary stormed up and down Chihuahua, Coahuila, Durango, and Sonora. His madcap
raids generated a crazy romance in the sleeping minds
of the little people who lived in despair and loneliness
far in the desert areas of his terrain. He broke the tedium
of their endless hours; he brought the jeweled glint of
mad excitement to their somber eyes. However *gringos*
regard him, the Mexicans have made him a champion
of the lowly. In their opinion, even his most bloodthirsty
deeds were justified. To see the Villa remembered in
Mexico, one must look at him through the eyes of the
peones.

To see the *hombre* remembered in the United States,
one must view him through the eyes of a different race,
an act which involves some readjustment of focus. After
Villa left the wildwood to enter the Revolution, he became the center of widespread American interest. Now
his behavior was closely scrutinized; his victories in
Chihuahua and his defeat at Celaya were documented

by American newsmen. This part of his epic, nonetheless, did not crystallize into a straight chronicle. The newsmen seldom interviewed the people who knew Villa, and so they gossiped with their friends about their own experiences with him. His subsequent attack on Columbus, New Mexico, and his flight from General Pershing likewise had a solid historical basis, which soon was revised in *corridos* and *cuentos* to depict him, as before, on the heroic scale. In order to present the complete Villa, the facts of his life, exceptional in themselves, need to be correlated with the feats attributed to him in songs and stories, as well as by the various persons whom he met on both sides of the border. His epic is essentially an oral history, in which the report, rather than the documented fact, was nearer to the spirit of the man and often quite as accurate.

The puzzle of Villa, who lived as a real person but who died a myth, may be unriddled by distinguishing his early outlawry as a legend and his leadership of the Revolution as a fact.

CHAPTER 2

Alias Pancho Villa

In the small Durango settlement of Rio Grande, hundreds of miles below the river of the same name, Doroteo Arango was born. Doroteo! What a name for a brown boy destined to make history as the fiercest leader of the Revolution! No wonder he changed his name to the more resounding Pancho Villa.

The parents of Doroteo were *peones* who lived on the ranch owned by the *hacendado* Don Arturo López Negrete—*peones* who knew poverty, disease, and belly hunger. Doroteo's father, Augustín Arango, comforted the mother, Micaela Arambula, after her legal husband had deserted her. One of his grandparents, on his father's side, was said to have been Jesus Villa, a descendant of a celebrated outlaw of earlier times, named Pancho Villa. On the night of Doroteo's birth, in 1878, a severe thunderstorm occurred. During the lightning, the evening star Venus changed its size and color, its shape and course. This storm people afterwards interpreted as an omen from the heavens, signifying the trouble ahead for the newborn son.

The Arango family, at Hacienda Rio Grande, lived in servility, an undistinguished segment of a large community. Theirs was a constricted world, a little *pueblo* surrounded by the towering peaks of the Sierra Madre.

8

A broad but shallow river, the diminutive Rio Grande of Durango, gave the place its name; its waters, browned with sediment of earth and leaves, enriched the farming lands which provided a livelihood for don and *peon* alike.

From his mother, Pancho sometimes heard of the great river at El Paso, the Rio Grande del Norte. But most of the time he labored with the peasants, tilling the rich soil. They planted cotton, which the don sold for a good profit. They raised their own simple provender, corn and beans, so that they proved of no expense to the ranch owner. Life on the ranch meant an endless round of ploughing, planting, hoeing, and harvesting. Don Arturo López Negrete, in whose person their sun centered, was absolute lord, absolute master.

A few things the boy learned at the ranch. For the Arangos, daily living spelled manual toil, the laborers being treated as little different from domestic animals. Both men and animals worked the farms to justify their existence. Since there was offered no opportunity really to educate the children, not much attempt was made to do so. In a word, the rigidity of caste offered no prospects for the lowly *peon*. To him, initiative was unknown. He grew fat and sluggish, eating *tortillas* and *frijoles*. While the caste system fed his belly, it robbed him of his dreams.

What did the peasant laborers do? On weekdays they worked from gray sunup past violet twilight into the dark purple of evening. After working all day in the fields, they had other chores to perform. The farm animals had to be fed and watered. Fat cows had to be milked. White or speckled eggs had to be gathered from the nests, in which the blue egg of a wild duck occasionally appeared. Kindling wood had to be cut for the fires to take the chill off the *adobe* rooms at night and in the crisp, cold mornings of Durango. Then they had their own suppers, but only after choice foods had been carried to the family kitchen of Don Arturo López Negrete. Except for Sundays, when the family of López Negrete turned out for church services in their finest clothes, one day became almost exactly like the next. Religion left Doroteo untouched, unmoved. He went to church only when forced to and then lounged in a place set apart for the lowly *peones*. This he resented. In many ways he preferred the tedium of weekdays to a Sunday dominated, not so much by the priest, as by the *hacendado*.

"*Mañana!*"

Once, a strange thing happened in the lumber town of Madera, Chihuahua; the people lost all record of time. It was during the Revolution, and the telephone and telegraph lines had been torn down by the rebels. As a train had not passed through there in six months, the people became accustomed to letting things slip by and thought nothing about it. They finally got the telegraph wires up again and wired El Paso to find out the hour of the day, the day of the week, and what date and month of the year it was. Nobody had been sufficiently interested to keep a count while they remained cut off from the outside world. They had simply lost all record of time. Such were those who nurtured and reared the great bandit of the border, in an atmosphere so remote from the realities of the twentieth century that even time could not intrude upon them.

How did Doroteo differ from the rest? Was there a reason why he, a submerged, unidentified figure among the sleeping masses, proved able to rise above circumstances and to cheat fate?

Possibilities abound, for the hero's subsequent triumphs were explained in many ways. Perhaps his independence of spirit could be traced to his real father. The man was not Augustín Arango but a rich Spanish nobleman. His mother, Micaela Arambula, came to her husband as a woman with a past. She had known a secret lover, who may or may not have become her legal husband. In many quarters, the suspicion lingered that he was a proud aristocrat and that in his veins ran the blue blood of nobility, a blood which set this son above the average peasant and destined him from the start for a grand future. Children with mixed blood were then not uncommon, and words in the folk song *"Boanerges"* might well have applied to Doroteo:

> My poor mother murmured comfortingly ....
> She said that through my throbbing veins
> Coursed a swift torrent of royal blood.

His personal appearance gave credence to the allegation, for he was a stolid Indian within but a light-skinned Mexican, of smiling mien, outside. His hair and mustache, kinky rather than straight, were brown with a reddish tint. Adenoids prevented his lips from closing completely, and he had a look as if he were always smiling.

The *peones* liked to describe him as an unspoiled child of nature. He was not, however, abjectly illiterate, since he could both read and write. This much and more he may have learned in the village Catholic school. It was his enemies, seeking to discredit him, who impugned his birth and upbringing, delineating him as an ignoramus. Colloquial and ungrammatical expressions, it is true, comprised the better part of his vocabulary, yet always he talked with a compelling fervor. His half-Indian heredity led him to speak a kind of "picture" language, so that he did not talk beyond the comprehension of his rustic, untutored listeners. Influential in winning him friends, Doroteo's rude speech helped to render him memorable to everybody who heard him talk.

Doroteo, as a youth, understood the hidden secrets of nature and wild animal life, in the uncanny ways of Indians. His matchless cunning suggests constantly that his chief forebears were tricky Indians. What he once fully learned, he never forgot. His sharp alertness, accordingly, developed into that of the trained hunter. His accurate marksmanship enabled him to fire with effect on the blue quail, which, quick as a flash, were at wing and away. His powers of observation were those of a scout who could kick into a dung heap and tell by its wetness how recently horses had passed along the trail. Through such practical experience he gained that uncommon knowledge which is the sixth sense. Like an animal, he could smell water at a distance, read the broken cry of the *paloma,* the gray dove, as a warning that intruders approached, see, behind a brown mesquite bush choked with heavy vines, the cool, sequestered cave hidden to other human view. The boy from Durango was nobody's fool.

While living on the ranch, this boy with the big brown eyes—and the uneven, yellow teeth—grew fond of animals. He had a pet dog or two and a pet burro. In his spare hours he chopped wood in the heavily timbered country of Durango and dreamed of buying a horse of his own. The kindling which he cut was easy to sell to the neighboring farmers. He became a *leñero,* a seller of bundles of wood. It took him quite a long time to save the money, but one day he had enough—and he brought a brown pony home with him. Now that he had a *caballo,* Doroteo explored places which beforehand were inaccessible to him. He rode far into the Sierra Madre. In the heart of the "Mother Mountains" he saw sights foreign to most human eyes, secure hiding places for stolen loot, strangely grotesque plants like the giant saguaro cactus.

Early, Doroteo Arango learned to conceal his cwn emotions; later he became an artist at camouflage. He could skip away into the mountains without leaving a trail behind. If he stole a fat beef and roasted it, he dug a hole in the ground for the carcass and left no evidence of his theft for the ranchers to complain of. And when he had a fine horse under him, he simply could not be caught. This man was able to vanish as completely as a phantom, into the hills.

Villa loved a good *caballo.* Horses were actually a necessary adjunct to him. To ride forever in a wild, headlong gallop—to pace with punctilious rhythm as though on parade—to loll at rest in the saddle while talking with his *compañeros*—these were for him the grand experiences! To see the young Villa was to behold the horseman. Proudly he straddled the mount, grandly it moved beneath him. So combined, they made an impressive picture. Of neither past nor future, this *vaquero* looked like the perfect horseman. Villa the horseman was liquid motion, and later people dubbed him *"El Centauro del Norte."*

But, as a boy, Doroteo Arango spent all his spare time with the little brown pony. It was a fine little horse, swifter than wind. Once upon a time he met Don Benito, a rich farmer of the neighboring El Dorado Ranch, who had with him his celebrated racer *"El Relampago,"* a horse as fast as lightning. Benito challenged Doroteo, then fifteen years old, to a contest. A moment before starting, the boy patted his horse and addressed him as "Little Friend."

Doroteo said: *"Amigito,* you must win this race. My *madre* is sick, and I need the *dinero* to help her. Please don't fail me, and I promise that if you win I will always take care of you and also give you a good name."

In the race which followed Doroteo's brown pony outran the more famous *"El Relampago."* True to his promise, the boy thanked his *caballo* and ever afterwards took proper care of him. Since the pony had won the race when the money was urgently needed, Doroteo gave him a fine name. He called him *"Buena Suerte,"* which in English means "Good Luck."

Always he kept his love of horses, Arabians, blue Appaloosas, black Morgans, and palominos. He preferred a white horse like his stallion, *"Siete Leguas."* A *corrido* told how this famous horse, called "Seven Leagues" in English, would stop and neigh when he heard a train whistle. It is said on the border that if any kind of mount struck his fancy, he would go to extremes to get the animal. One amusing *cuento,* told about him in after years, concerned a clever little ranch girl named Helena Lovrett, daughter of a hated *gringo.* It was she who prevented him from stealing the kingly, midnight-black stallion *"El Rey de la Noche."* When Villa raided the *rancho* in her father's absence, the pretty child walked over to the *bravo* and asked him if he wanted to see a beautiful and valuable horse.

"*Sí, niña linda,*" he said, "I want very much to do so."

What little Helena brought him was a painted cardboard pony, which she presented to him. Villa, who apparently loved children more than horses, accepted the gift in fine spirit.

As a youngster on the ranch, Doroteo spent the endless days tramping in the woods, with cock fights and horse races, but hot rancor burned in his heart. On the outside he wore the mask of an Indian, but inside he stayed always tense. Always he looked far into the distance, listening to sounds unheard by others. Sometimes an anger like madness seethed in him as turbulently as the waters welling in the Rio Grande when on a rampage. All of his youthful companions grew afraid of him when his black eyes hardened to red coals and stared straight through them. For he was more than they, and they surely must have known it.

In those early years, Doroteo must have sensed that there was a greater heritage awaiting him than the life of futility that had been bequeathed him within the confines of Don Arturo López Negrete's feudal estate. This extraordinary young *peon,* whose blood cried out for freedom, must have known intuitively that his future— and his freedom—lay inseparably intertwined with the rugged, untamed peaks of the blue and green Sierra Madre. They betokened adventure and release from the ranch at Rio Grande. Doroteo Arango heard the insistent, steady call of the Mexican wilderness, and the Indian inside him listened and heard.

CHAPTER 3

Avenger and Fugitive

Pride in his pretty sister Mariana made Doroteo Arango an outlaw. His pride in her, and in family honor, meant more than life to him. Her sad fall was one day to affect his whole future.

The Arango family lived in simplicity and poverty, but Doroteo grew big and proud. Besides his father, his mother, and himself, there were two daughters and two other sons. The boy next to him in age was Hipolito, and the third son was Antonio. The two girls were Mariana, at times called Anita, and Mariquita. Since Doroteo was the oldest son, Hipolito and Antonio naturally tagged along after him, each a trifle awed and frightened by their big brother striding ahead. This family of five children meant hard toil in the fields for the parents and careful saving of their few resources. They did all right so long as Augustín Arango stayed well and hearty, but fortune struck them a staggering blow when he fell ill, quickly grew worse, and died. This unexpected tragedy left Doroteo with heavy responsibilities. Being then too young to stifle his emotions, he became prostrate with grief. The thought of his mother, robbed of her mate and bent with despondency, overcame him in floods of love and pity. He now drew his brothers and sisters more closely to him than ever before. Like the man he knew

he must become, he regarded the two little girls with unusual tenderness, because henceforth he must be their
provider as well as their protector. And the children had
to be fed—fed immediately. His own scanty schooling
must be discontinued so that the others could have decent
clothes in which to go to school. The staggering question
facing him was whether he could earn enough money on
the ranch to keep things going. He soon learned he could
not.

To Don Arturo López Negrete and especially to his
degenerate son, Leonardo, the situation gave signs of
ripening to their liking. Young López Negrete burned
with lust for Mariana and knew he could force himself
on her when she began to starve and sicken. Neither old
nor young López Negrete ever thought that Doroteo
might be able to provide for his loved ones. They did
not see him as he truly was.

Poverty forced Doroteo, inexperienced head of a
household, to look immediately for a better job. Lured
by the promise of a livable wage, he went to work on a
neighboring *rancho,* where he hoped to solve his prob-
lems. He left the *hacienda* without permission, and Arturo López Negrete maddened with resentment. Doroteo was brought home in bonds and flogged without
mercy, the heavier scars accompanying him to the grave.
His youthful dream of succoring his family lay in ruins.
Doroteo must have lost his stomach and vomited copi-
ously on that blindingly hot day as the whip battered his
raw flesh wide open to sizzle in the sun. He fried in the
hell of feudalism, and his gorge rose at the injustice. The
spirit flooding him was that of some aristocratic forebear
or that of the old outlaw Pancho Villa, *"El Viejo,"*
to whom he now knew he must be related through

his grandfather, Jesus Villa. His eyes flared; his lips trickled redly where he bit them; and his ears drowned themselves in thunder. The deafening roar he heard was the full-throated cry for freedom, the firm conviction that he would not relive his mistakes. In naked degradation, he lost his old soul. Seeing his young body carved to fit the feudal mould, he found the true salvation of belief in self. Nobody ever again made the mistake of thinking him a slave. Nobody ever again lived to boast that he had flogged Pancho Villa.

After the wounds healed, he emerged a new man ready to tackle the hardness of the world. The López Negretes had not conquered. Doroteo was alive, wasn't he? Someday he would return to fight again.

Regretfully he parted from his helpless, tearful mother; from the gawky, growing brothers; from the two sisters whose warm beauty glowed in the darkness, radiant and alive. It tore at his vitals to leave his pretty sister Mariana. He would be seeing them again, he said; he never could be so far away as they might suppose. It was *adios* for a little while, not farewell forever. Stung to his innards, literally burning in anger and pity, he rode furiously away, he and *Buena Suerte* galloping unnoticed far into the black Durango night. It was a dangerous thing to do. He could be branded a fugitive and permanently ruined. Off into the distance, the hapless *muchacho* sped into the mysterious night.

But he had not gained freedom, for the López Negretes found him easily. He was driving a freight wagon between Buenacevi and Chihuahua City, and minding his own business. On a false charge of thievery he was easily punished, convicted, jailed. Don Arturo López Negrete could show the light to him. Could he not see that he was the hapless pawn of fate? Well, let him think it over, rot a while in jail, rub shoulders with stinking, hardened criminals. Let him breathe the filth and taste the dirt; let him vegetate among the vermin. The long arm of the law reached out to erase the rebel's spirit. Like a heavy rod of rigid steel, it banged down hard across his cranium. Only a thick skull would be untaught by that, Don Arturo reasoned.

In jail, Doroteo barely had sense enough to wait out his sentence. Rebellion rankled deep within him. At first he drifted among the prisoners aimlessly. There was absolutely nothing to do in the dirty *cárcel*. Amid slime and filth he and the other prisoners rotted away, doing nothing. They joined into bands and stole cigarettes from new prisoners or begged them from the few visitors who came to the *cárcel,* which was a rambling, unsanitary building, with a few underground cells for hardened criminals. The prisoners beneath the earth suffered from lack of sunlight or a kind of vitamin deficiency. Those who stayed over-long in the darkened cells grew semi-blind, their skin becoming so dry that it flaked off. These unfortunates always hungered for any kind of green vegetables. They would trade a cigarette any day for a green *chili* pepper. When Doroteo first entered the jail, he got into a fight and was himself stuck into one of the "hell holes" for a week. After that he kept his wits about him, never pestering the other prisoners again over cigarettes or *chili* peppers. Now he tried something new, and on the outside wore a friendly look, no matter how he rankled inwardly. Soon he became a friend of old prisoners and newcomers alike, spending most of his time flat on his back, in the shade, listening to the yarns of older, more experienced *bandidos*. Then one day he heard of a man whose exploits gave him an idea. He listened closer, fascinated.

"They told me," he said afterwards, "about famous outlaws who robbed the rich to aid the poor. One of the outlaws, a grand *bandido* called Parra, impressed me very much. I swore then that I'd be like him some day."

Now that he had his vision, he endured the jail at Buenacevi. A Spanish don had made him an outcast; now the military authorities, in charge of the public jail, set about making him an outlaw. All this time a plan began to formulate itself in his head. Inwardly loathing and despising their very names, he swore on both Spaniards like Arturo López Negrete and Federalists like his jailors a vengeance which he never forgot. So long as he rotted away in prison, he kept his enmity well in the background and thought constantly of the *bandido* Ignacio Parra.

When he gained his freedom, Doroteo emerged with a dream in his head. To external eyes, he appeared chastened and preoccupied. He was. He found it exhilarating to breathe again the sharp air blown down from the wonderful Sierra Madre, to take a place once more under the splendid sun. There was much to do. He must stay apart from the ranch where he had been cut off and branded an outcast, yet he must soon communicate with his mother and with his sister Mariana. The tempo of his being had slowed to a halt while he languished in the *cárcel*.

Now time hurtled by. He had to have a nest egg and on nearby ranches and in Chihuahua City repeatedly asked for a job. The *rancheros* would not hire him because they knew he was an outcast from the Hacienda Rio Grande. Life, he found again, could be hard, cruelly hard. Somehow he made money in the city; and somehow he managed to send a few savings home. It was so good to be free that he sometimes almost knew happiness.

Then love came. The first thought entering his mind was to hurry back to his mother, to tell her the happy news that he now was in love with a girl he had met in Chihuahua City. Her name was María Luz Corral, and, best of all, she had promised to marry him. What lovely times she and his adored sister Mariana could have together! His imagination brimmed with prospects. As his loved one was a beauty, his veins throbbed with liquid fire. He felt a new optimism and assured himself that all yet might be well. Maybe, he reasoned, he had himself erred somewhere. The injustices he had suffered rankled less and less: Forgive? Never! Forget? Yes! Every day it became easier and easier to forget. Besides, it was high time that he was making a place for himself in the world. Perhaps, after all, he could become a tradesman in the city, a freighter or a butcher. Perhaps he could forget the old troubles with the López Negretes, that were his nightmare. Like all country boys, he thrilled to his core at the prospect of making good in a big city. His first love inspired him gloriously.

Exactly then the letter came. He had been keeping up with his family, sending his mother a part of his earnings, writing her that his health continued fine, inquiring warmly about his brothers and sisters, including a kiss or two for the virgin Mariana. Immediately he sensed the injury. He knew. Why read over the mother's inexact wording—the halting hint of honor lost? He knew, and was weak with the knowledge. The picture of the don's degenerate son swept full before his eyes and blinded them. Mariana! Mariana! Mariana! Another picture thrust itself before him, a scene of her ripening olive body, her nude body two shades lighter than gold —all its treasures ransacked, ravaged, plumbed to a source bespangled with blood. In one moment all his youth was dead and gone and buried. Each time he thought of the stained body, he trembled from top to toe. A small crevasse seemed to break slightly open somewhere at the top of his head, creasing the middle of his skull. His blood throbbed as madly as the waters of the Rio Bravo in flood time.

That night, riding the long stretch between Chihuahua City and Hacienda Rio Grande, he calmed down. During the night, dark and bitter cold, he reminisced mournfully. Childhood memories thronged his mind, with Mariana's face constantly growing clearer until the other faces blotted out and disappeared. It seemed as though she had died. He saddened now more than when his father had passed away. It was the difference, the difference! How rotton, vilely rotten, it all was. She was dishonored irreparably. How sad—how unutterable and vacant the sadness. His mind revolved everywhere. Maybe a mistake had occurred. It was untrue—and his heart leaped. It was true—and his heart fell. The pain generated itself in waves, starting and stopping and starting again. A nipping wind whipped at him. The night air, growing steadily colder, reached freezing. He grew weak from nervous exhaustion; he felt the bitter cold curdle the strong milk of his marrow. Then the pain receded. Now it did not stop and then start as before. During the long, bleak ride home his anger never stopped boiling.

As soon as he arrived, Doroteo screamed: *"Donde está Mariana?"* "Where is my little sister?"

Then he saw at a glance that she was not at home. His mother tried vainly to stop him, to inform him that she had gone to the village for supplies.

"Be careful, my son," his mother sobbed, "for she will not tell me the devil's name."

He knew who *"el diablo"* was, and Mariana would tell Doroteo, he swore to himself. When she came in, he hugged and kissed her, saw the heartbreak in her eyes, kissed dry her tear-wet face. He drew her to a place aside; from her trembling lips he heard in privacy of the brutal assault by Leonardo. She pleaded with him, dropping to her bended knees. But in vain. His course was set. The remainder of that interminable night he waited on time, which so often before had hurried him.

Far off, beyond the far distant tops of the Sierra Madre, dawn at last broke. After what seemed an infinity it became bright daylight, yellow, warm, full. Looking outside the house, he saw, high over the waist-high grass, droves of blue quail begin to dot the sky, almost darkening the yellow sun in wedge after wedge of indigo feathers. Only a little afterwards Doroteo rode to find Leonardo, and it happened that they met at the crossroads. Doroteo dismounted and held the reins of his horse carelessly with his left hand.

"Look here, Leonardo," the injured brother accosted him. "I want to trade words with you."

"Yes, what's on your mind? Why do you wish to speak with me?" the scoundrel replied.

"Leonardo," said the proud Doroteo, "you have betrayed my sister. . . ."

"Why you dirty *peon*," angrily interrupted the Don, "how dare you talk to me in that manner. Get off this ranch *pronto* and stay off. Your sister lies."

With this last statement the raging Leonardo may have grabbed for his gun. If so, he was too slow, for Doroteo personified lightning with a pistol. Without drawing fire he drilled his man three times. Young López Negrete was dead before he sank to the earth. In the next moment Doroteo was back on his horse, galloping determinedly toward the far-off hills.

The primitive in Doroteo Arango had killed a man. It was his first murder, done to avenge the family honor. Henceforth he would be the hunted, not the hunter. To caste society his act represented a crime. Now he learned that it was one thing to be a runaway, another to be a prisoner, and quite yet another to be an outlaw. Hereafter he would kill and escape to kill again.

As he fled from the past, did he ask himself why Mariana, his *hermanita querida,* had not more carefully guarded her virtue? Did he realize that the terrible epithet of murderer would follow him for the rest of his days? Or did his pride reassert itself? He had shown them, hadn't he? What did he really do? The hot-blooded but sentimental Doroteo, whose firecracker temper was often followed by an opposite mood of copious weeping, now wept salty tears over the disgrace of his sister and the shock of killing his first victim. Finally he staunched his tears.

Afterwards the strong *caballo* beneath him plunged ever onward. A strange exhilaration began to stir within him comfortingly. How wonderful its welling. On the blackest day of his life, the spirit of Ignacio Parra soothed him. Before Doroteo, *alias* Pancho Villa forevermore, spread the plan he had formulated in prison of becoming a savior of poor families like his own that he now had to leave behind.

Meanwhile the symbolic Rio Grande trickled slowly through the desert. When it reached the mountains, waters sped from a thousand streamlets to fill its bed, and when it reached Santa Elena Canyon, the river became a raging torrent, roaring through the high rock-like walls on either bank until its bed broadened, its waters subsided. Then it returned again to a wide expanse of water steadily flowing toward the Gulf of Mexico.

The sorcery of tonic mountain air soon wrought a boy early in his 'teens from a craven into a bold fugitive. The *corrido En los montes mas remotos* described the plight of a man much like him.

> In the wilderness untrammelled,
> In the highest mountain crags,
> I'll hide myself,
> Where none will know I was guilty,
> For my great love of thee,
> Of such a crime.

CHAPTER 4

Birth of a Bandit

The murderer who sought refuge in the Sierra Madre was a primitive. Under better conditions, he would have grown into an undistinguished *peon,* fat and healthy. He had been forced into outlawry; he became a bandit through necessity. The symbol of flight, a fleeing toward or from something, reappeared throughout the remainder of his life as one of the best explanations of his entire personality. The rarest thing in the world for him was to trust anybody, either his leaders who took him into their company or his own tried and loyal *compañeros.* He made his cooks taste his food before he ate it; he slept safely at a distance, apart from his men, not because he demanded a special privilege, not because he swelled with pride as *El Jefe,* the big chief. After all, he had been shaken to his foundations by the dereliction of his own flesh and blood in the fall of his sister Mariana.

On the day of that first murder, immediately after the shooting, the fated man rode straight ahead. Vanishing from the *hacienda* at Rio Grande into the little-explored reaches of the Sierra Madre, Doroteo Arango choked with a sad memory, which droned in his thoughts like an old refrain.

I'll hide myself,
Where none will know I was guilty,
For my great love of thee,
Of such a crime.

He passed into hiding, safe from pursuers, among the verdant canyons of the Barranca del Cobre, that for long years before had been sanctuary for other marked, unfortunate men.

In blotting out his sister's smirch, he had acted upon primal impulses. At the same time, he probably had a plan in his mind when he acted, possibly already had plotted out his future movements during that memorable night before the killing. Basically Indian as he was, he must have realized that otherwise his chances for a clean break, for a complete escape, would have been pitifully slim. It is unthinkable that he did not look ahead. The repeated punishment meted out to him by old López Negrete would have taught him at least that much. He surely had thought about what hiding from the law meant and how he would be hunted again as soon as he slipped from the sanctuary of those uncharted mountains. In view of his admiration for the bandit Ignacio Parra, it is possible that he felt confident of being able to join with the outlaw breed and of easily losing his original identity among them. He may have thought far, far ahead, when he galloped off toward the towering, ragged hills, meaning all the time to meet there a *"grupo"* of those *compañeros* by prearranged appointment. However it occurred, his flight into the Sierra Madre ended in a rendezvous with destiny.

Upward, upward toward the heart of the forest ranges, the young outlaw climbed. Mesquite grass gave way to scrubby bush, which, in turn, gave way to finer and finer *piños* trees, as he ever upward climbed. He saw few birds, few animals. Once he passed a colony of running armadillos. Now and again he saw bright blue quail plummet into the bush; later he saw only eagles, wheeling high, and stinking vultures, immobile upon the weathered rocks. The insects looked the strangest: yellow beetles, purple fireflies, and especially blue grasshopper-like bugs with the brilliant reddish wings of iridescent butterflies. Later on, in the upper regions of the Barranca del Cobre, the air felt intensely cold. Riding along its rim, he looked five thousand feet down to the sweltering, fecund bottom of the teeming tropical Barranca below.

Pancho made the most of the short headstart which he had. Since the furor over the killing mounted quickly, the news spread far and wide. Leagues ahead of the buckskin-clothed *rurales* chasing him, he rode determinedly, making the best use of *Buena Suerte* and not burning him out all at once in a furious dash for cover. He had far to go, this lone horseman, riding past time into tomorrow. He must not wear out either his mount or, for that matter, himself. His chances were much better here than in the city, because he knew the lay of the western land and what to do to survive in rough country. He saw to it that his *caballo* was fed and watered. As best he could, he took care of himself, sleeping in deep caves protected from the chilling winds blowing up at night among the high Sierras, and hiding away, soft and sound, in warm darkness from the sharp eyes of the posse which followed miles and miles behind. During the day he ate the green, waxy mesquite bean, chewing at wild haws and purple berries till his lips reddened.

He wandered, on a brilliant moonlit midnight, into a weird part of the Sierra Madre, a terrain unfit for man, a place where there existed neither animals nor vegetables to eat. A full moon swung above on that midnight; it cast an eerie glow over the forest of cactus trees. Huge, flowering cactus plants, looking like high, skeletoned skyscrapers, gave him water but no food. The terrain spread out before him as a blackened, dangerous land. The small carnivorous plants he had seen once before in his youth, the pitcher plant and the Venus fly trap, here grew to giant proportions.

By the minute, his strength dwindled as his hunger mounted. He fought the growing menace of the two of them: weakening knees and a growling stomach. Eventually he came to a place where animal life again abounded, but for fear of giving his pursuers a tell-tale signal, he could not build a fire to cook a brush rabbit or a fat quail, either of which he easily might have caught under the cover of darkness. Furry and feathered things nestled undisturbed in the vast wilderness in which he traveled. The fathomless depths of Indian fortitude hardened him, wrought him into personification of will; and so he went yet farther onward, enduring the gnawing hunger that bit into his vitals and bent his middle, the ponderous weight of fatigue and exhaustion that burdened his bone. If his mind wandered, his nerves jerked him back to the center of consciousness. Besides, the terrain began to improve. There now were numerous signs of animal life. He made excellent time, riding into history and legend, and he kept gaining distance until at last he felt safe.

For food he once ate a tender brush rabbit that he caught. He skinned the animal and ate it raw. He wiped the blood from his mouth with a handful of oak leaves. He scrubbed his hands clean of the blackening blood in the soft, warm sand. At another time he ate *"dillo"* meat, pork of the desert, saving the hard armadillo armor for use as a canteen. The water in the streams of the Barranca del Cobre, to which he finally came, appeared green from copper deposits, but it was wet and cool. He gulped his fill of the emerald water.

Then one morning as the scarlet sun swung around, Doroteo Arango awoke with a start. Looming there above him stood Ignacio Parra! From the ground where Doroteo slept, the terrible specter towered to the skies.

"What's your name, *muchacho?*" the grand *bandido* asked.

Before he knew it Doroteo answered quickly, "Pancho Villa!"

The fierce Parra broke out in laughter. "You mean," he said, "the *bandido* of long ago?"

"His namesake," the boy retorted.

Parra was pleased by the quick reply the youngster gave him. He realized that the boy could think fast; immediately Parra liked him, whether he lied or not. Pancho Villa! What a name for a big overgrown boy asleep in the mountains. A place could surely be found in his bandit band for a lad like that.

"Look what I have found!" he cried out to his *compañeros.*

And then, as the grand *bandido* told them how he caught the boy asleep, all of them laughed uproariously. At the outlaw camp, Parra's return had brought the bandits to their feet, at attention. Then, after taking seats about the campfire, they listened to their *jefe's* adventure. And next, assuredly, the bandits made believe: the

boy's name savored of a marvelous possibility; they remembered an earlier bandit by that name and knew he
had left descendants. *"Pancho Villa!"* They went over
it among themselves. At first the fun-loving outlaws
probably twitted him by repeating the name, shouting to
the deaf, unreplying hills, *"Pancho Villa! El Niño!"*
Although they called him a child, some of them thought
of the youngster as the old Villa's grandson. Others simply had fun with him, screaming out to him as he per-
formed some task about the camp, *"Ola, Panchito,* bring
us wood for the fire! *Ola, Panchito,* let me see your gun"
—but finally they accepted him along with his sobriquet,
and even sympathized with him, exclaiming in lively
concert, *"Carramba,* Pancho, but you were right! And
your *'hermanita,'* Pancho Villa, was she *muy, muy
linda?"* In the dull days following a raid, they listened
about the campfire to the tragedy of his life. Tired of
seeing and hearing each other, the outlaws welcomed a
newcomer to the band.

Pancho Villa—the name stuck with him thereafter—
could spin a fine yarn. He made a good-natured member
of their fireside group. He could tell, in his repetitive
rural speech, tall adventures night after night. So he told
them, it is certain, what had happened. He was then a
newcomer, and the bandits grew sympathetic, exclaiming that here existed a fine tragedy all right, a happening
from real life. With many an oath and exclamation, they
cursed and cried about young López Negrete and Mariana. But after a space the tragedy grew cold, and the bandits then wanted to hear something new. Pancho could
tell them anything. Their leader, the bold *bandido,*
Parra, never had trouble getting the young *caballero* to
spin a tale as they sat in the flaring light of the campfire,

resting from the day's lucrative activities. All Parra
needed to do was to declare that he had heard it rumored
that Pancho Villa was a witty one, a prince among liars
—for Ignacio Parra could never forget, without chuck-
ling, how quick the young man's retort had flashed on
that day of their first meeting. It must have been true,
what Parra said, for Pancho could really pass the time
away by relating to the hardened bandits his fine yarns.
The young Pancho, to whom exaggeration came naturally, commenced with a narrative, half-formed in his
mind as soon as he started, of daring escapes he had made
from his enemies.

"In the year 1896," Panchito must have begun, making his tale sound like the truth as best he could. "I first
had to run away from home to escape the *rurales*. I ran
as fast as I could toward the blue mountains, far away
there in the distance. I had heard then of Parra; I knew
that he lived there the free life of a bandit. I myself was
too young at the time to roam in the mountains; I found
the going hard. For a while I lived in great danger, with
the *rurales* hot upon my trail. Not knowing the mountains, I hid in the canyons, in Devil's Canyon, the Canyon of Witches, and the Canyon of Hell. I became
almost *loco* when they caught me, from fear and home-
sickness gone out of my head," and maybe here he struck
the tangled thatch of hair which looked to a casual ob-
server as though it were curly when it stood up un-
combed and mussed, as it generally was; and maybe then
he said, continuing provocatively: "because at that time
you see, I had no *amigos*. It was the *rurales* who caught
me and put me in the big prison at San Juan del Rio. *Si,
compañeros,* the food was terrible; *ay,* my friends, the
straw pallet was wormy and smelled.

"All the day the doors on the jail stood wide open; all the time the guards were sleeping or drunk. Yes, *amigo,* I knew *la ley fuga,* knew if they saw me escaping I would be shot like the brown rabbit as I ran. But one day I found a *metate* they had left where they ground corn. *Ay, sí,* it was hard and heavy; *ay, ay,* it felt smooth next my palm. I picked up the stone and balanced it; up and down the *metate* went in my hand; and then bang! I let the guard have it. He lay dead with a crack in his skull. Pancho did not slip this time; you know Pancho did not slip. It was just at that time," he concluded, maybe eyeing Parra to see if he drew pleasure or unhappiness from the tale, "that I first met two of you *caballeros* who are seated with me here right now. Who do you suppose I met in the mountains but those two *amigos* so restless over there? The one, he is Refugio Alvarado; the other, he is Antonio Parra, seated next to our leader nearest the fire."

And there, perhaps, the story ended. Some of the tales which people later told about Villa, he surely first told of himself. For a season, maybe longer, the bandits must have listened and wondered. That the *muchacho* was glib, they could see. Perhaps Parra stopped him, *"ya basta,"* "it is enough." Then they got down to business, planned out a raid before the coming dawn. Establishing himself every day more and more as a real *compañero,* Pancho always looked twice as serious as the others, feeling his old dream begin its palpitations anew. He now sensed within him temblors that mingled with a primitive stirring. Like an unbroken stallion, he stirred inside him with the mad plunging, the crazy kicking of a bandit being born. Then he sensed something else, something opposite and different. The pugnacity remained, but he now commenced to feel silkily feline. In every fiber of his taut body he felt like the tawny, tight-skinned, yellow-eyed pumas that he had seen quietly stalking their prey in the Barranca del Cobre. Felinely he quieted on the outside while a saffron ball of fire burned larger and hotter inside him until his firecracker temper went off, until he pounced outside his own velvet skin with angry joy. He became Pancho the Puma!

Parra's outlaw band crept near their prey under cover of night. At the first crack of dawn, they dashed from their hiding place and, firing their pistols and yelling *gritos* at the top of their lungs, pounced upon the luckless train or stage before them. The din of pistol shots and the noise of their blood-curdling cries paralyzed the trainmen or drivers. They moved in a hurry, without camouflage, unmasked. Their raids happened so quickly that the prey was left dazed, speechless, unable when questioned to say exactly what had happened, capable of recalling amid the then deafening roar that confounded them only scraps of things—at first, now that the victims tried to recount it, the pounding of thunderous hooves, the *loco* cries of the bandits, the screaming and shooting, and yet everything had seemed confusedly simultaneous; intermittent or continuous, they knew not which. The bandits looted so completely and so soon that a brief moment after they departed, their victims could not realize what had befallen them. The whole fracas assumed the construction of a nightmare that could not be nailed too hard to certain reality. What had happened? The group with whom Pancho operated were so thorough, not even the people who were there to see it knew really what this thundering pack of *lobos* had done.

What thrills resulted from both the raid and its sequel! Not in counting the gold. The money seemed the least important of all, for there remained more of it, much more of it to be taken in Mexico. It was not even the mad daring, for there were deeds more daring. The hottest thrill came from the spectacular excitement of murder. Murder made the pulse beat faster; murder made the head throb grandly. The experience—that was it, and wisdom gained from the experience. The mad careening of Pancho's *Buena Suerte,* of Parra's massive blue Appaloosa with a star in her forehead, named *Estrella Azul,* set his wits awhirl with ecstasy. *Carramba!* To be honest, it grew into the realization that all things sprang naturally. Murder was so easy; and it made his temperature rise intoxicatingly.

Talking it over later, Parra frequently complimented Pancho on an act that appeared like a stroke of inspiration. But the action had not come from inspiration. Pancho Villa was no genius. He continued to be a primitive, acting as a primitive. And he certainly was that, all right. And murder was easy, so easy, as easy as breathing.

And so he killed some of the times. But it was done for others; it was done to protect other people. Pancho Villa would be a *bandido* different from Ignacio Parra, different from all bandits everywhere. He felt warm, silken, sentimental, and full of big saline tears. He would help the poor little people of the Republic, that nobody else helped. Also, he would have lots of horses— maybe an Appaloosa like Parra's! But afterwards, when he thought of young López Negrete's rape of his *hermanita querida,* he became dry as bone, hard as steel, and hotly blind in both eyes. He could kill man upon man like the young Negrete. Always afterwards he felt unworried, calm—relaxed. Always afterwards he slept like a baby. He shot somebody just like that, and a little time afterwards he began to get sleepy, began to dream his wonderful dream.

A voice, perhaps that of his grandfather Villa, came then from the mist and told him to listen to the *grán bandido*. To become a hero of a people, he must learn all Parra knew. He must remember what Parra said, what Parra did, how Parra rode, how Parra lived, how Parra fought. For one of these days Parra would die in hot and bloody action. Since everything came naturally to him, Pancho learned twice as rapidly as any other of his *compañeros*. Off in Nature's own wilderness, he did this and he did that, and things were so with him—were so much better than they had ever been before—that he breathed in self-reliance and exhaled friendliness. He exuded such confidence that all the men became his entirely. Also Pancho, without thanking his stars, went ever upward in the estimate of Ignacio Parra, until he became Parra's righthand man. At the back of Pancho's head, especially when he thought of the *grán bandido's* massive blue Appaloosa mare, the idea of one day surpassing even Parra himself began to ferment.

Ay, that Pancho Villa could talk!—and work hard. However, when he sank into silence, he was most effective. Ponderous and heavy, he looked as though he were deliberating fateful decisions, as though his heavy Indian face had endured everything. When everybody talked and jabbered and gesticulated wildly, Pancho Villa grew silent. He practiced every cunning trick of that wisdom of wisdom—silence. Like a sullen puma, he studied how to sway men and to dominate them. *Ay,* the roles this *peon* outlaw had in his repertory! When all the other short-thinking outlaws rambled about, the impassive Pancho stood apart. Soft and smooth and snug, the magic mantle of silence moved, meandered, and settled about him.

Of course all of the outlaws had women, some of whom later became *"soldaderas"* in the fight against the Federal *rurales*. They made raids at times, not for food nor money, but for girls. A band of outlaws would be sent to the outskirts of a town to harry and plunder, to draw its protectors to the fray. When the citizens rode from their houses to protect the entrance of their town, Villa, forgetful of the rape of his sister, learned to take the unprotected women left at home. Mostly they took young *señoritas,* plump fourteen-year-old ones. After that the *bandidos* debauched; still later they rested and slept.

During the interim between raids Pancho Villa sought quiet, slumbering apart, face downward, the sleep of an animal. Trigger nerves demanded much rest, hours torn from the clock. When he was not raiding, something seemed really gone out of him. He needed a "battery charge." He ate, rested, slept, woke, and slept again. Around and around the clock, Pancho Villa slept, recharging that brain of his constantly.

How is a bandit born? On the outside he is born as smooth as velvet; on the inside he is born as full of tremblings as an earthquake. He knew he would be bad. Before the dawn, he would be eager to start out, longing in his vitals for the *señoritas*. Then finally Parra would ask if he was ready. Ready? *Carramba,* he was ready and waiting!

With the lightning thrust that so often comes with the dangerous life, Pancho's fortunes abruptly changed.

Once a stage traveling toward a mining company carried a payroll of $100,000. Unknown to Parra and his favored henchman Villa, the stage was packed, not with the usual guard or two, but with a number of suspicious officers and Federal soldiers. The outlaw band literally fell upon the coach, which promptly retaliated by emptying a squad of crack riflemen. Amid the quick gunfire and the horsemen's wheeling, the sky exploded. The bandits that day paid with blood for the payroll they took. Ignacio Parra met his death early in the fighting, being shot from his Appaloosa horse, that had tried to break away in fear to head for the hills. Villa led the rally and reassembled the band under his own leadership. That night he rode back to camp on dead Parra's horse, *Estrella Azul*.

The return of the bandits to camp was their saddest, for in the death of Parra they had lost their original founder. The bandits faced the need, with the aid of Villa, of fitting the pieces into place in order to remain banded together. Pancho represented the logical successor to the revered Parra, and so it was he who took over the leadership.

Did he now miss that familiar interruption by Parra? Possibly the spirit of old Ignacio nudged Villa's fine friend Juan Salas, urging him to speak.

"*Ola,* Pancho," the ghost of Parra made Juan Salas say, "we are men with *mucho dinero;* it all goes to waste while we linger here. Why should we remain in mourning? The *rurales* but bury their soldier dead. You could go by the safety of darkness; your true men would guard you well. You waste the night talking and bragging; your little *paloma* is lonely when she is not with her brave bandit."

Upon some such occasion Villa may have nodded in agreement with his *amigo,* Juan Salas. There were, mingled with the turbulence of the constant raiding parties, many sentimental hours. When the opportunity offered, he catapulted from the hills in sudden descent upon the Hacienda Rio Grande to visit his mother and the youngsters. Yet later on, he knew, approvingly or otherwise, that his brothers and sisters moved to Chihuahua City and left the poor *madre* at home, because in the old Indian tradition she could not be brought to part with a place so full of memories. He endured the greatest grief that a strong man experiences the day his mother died. When the news of her death reached him, the grief-stricken man succumbed to tears at the hard trick of Fate which had kept him from her in her last long hours alone. His followers saw the woeful spectacle that he presented on that bitter winter day as he stood beside his horse moaning, whimpering like a whipped and beaten boy. Sad hours had their place upon the chronometer in the clockless eternities of his bandit life.

Love for María Luz Corral naturally strengthened in him after his mother's death. The loss of one woman's love brought to him a concentration of love upon another woman, a love that he learned to understand, to cherish, because it grew and grew. He came to love Luz with an abiding passion.

Perhaps it was Thomas Urbina or Martin Lopez or, more likely, Juan Salas who transformed Pancho into action and broke him from the spell of reminiscing which caused such anguished aching, such longing. Then with sharp blasts on a whistle, he headed straight to the listening horses. Probably he chose the Appaloosa that stood listening nearby, ready and impatient. He and his eager band of outlaws, spurring away into the gathering darkness for Chihuahua City, made a rousing picture. They galloped down the road to adventure and tender romance.

There is no tree but casts a shadow,
    And no maiden, now and forever, but is loving.

CHAPTER 5

A Gay Caballero

Although he adored his Luz, Pancho Villa's career was full of erotic adventure. He had at least three legal wives: Soledad Seanez, Estroberta Rentería, and María Luz Corral. He did not fancy the slender *gringa* type but liked a girl with plenty of meat on her. But despite his many amorous experiences, he had but one abiding lover, María Luz.

When the young man Villa fell in love, he experienced something which the common bandits never felt, something as free as the air, as certain as the midnight sky with its fateful Lucero star. *Amor!* The cold-blooded Indian part of Villa stayed at camp when he was fired with love for Luz and rode away to the city. Compared to the rest of the bandits, he behaved like a man apart, the lover transcendent. When in the freshness of love for Luz, he felt much better than at any other time: the black thoughts receded as *amor* welled within his heart, oiling his pride, nurturing his narcissism. When Pancho Villa fell deeply in love, he left his cold aboriginal Indian self at home; he became Spanish, warm and emotional. During such happy hours everything tasted *dulce, muy dulce*—sweeter than soft brown cactus candy. The sweets of life belonged to him. His love, strong enough to make him attack or kill whoever sought to be a rival, burned like a red-hot coal of fire.

As a laughing young lover, Pancho Villa made a striking figure. In his younger days, before he affected the mustache which hid his adenoidal mouth but drooped and trailed away too much, many people regarded him as particularly handsome. He had a splendid physique, with large firm shoulders; he stood about six feet in height, being somewhat taller and better-proportioned than the average man. Before his weakness for murdering got the better of him, Pancho Villa had warm brown eyes that looked about him steadily and full. His manners always reflected the best traditions. He was oily, his speech sprinkled with *"por favor"* this and *"por favor"* that. Long after he had, in the war, become drunk with his narcissism and had heard the voices prophesying the splendor of his destiny, he could and did impress suspicious *gringo* news reporters with his charm, his excellent display of taste, and his practical view of urgent military matters. Pancho evidently had been endowed at birth with the precious sense called timing. When he wanted to, he could persuade his most skeptical critic to see the reason why a brutal action had been necessary to save time or to protect the lives of others. Such talents in a handsome man would naturally overpower the women, both the *señorita* and her *dueña,* if she were lucky enough to have a chaperon along to shield her.

His role as a musician also made him dangerous with the ladies. He played the guitar and other musical instruments but grew fondest of singing, ringing out the honeyed love songs with a round full voice. He must have made an impressive sight, this melodious Mexican *caballero,* at rest on his horse while his *canción* filled the resounding air. When Luz Corral, his *paloma,* drew near, he accented and prolonged the dulcet notes. Luz had for him the fragrance of apple blossoms in the spring; he simply welled with song at the scent of her. The gift of song came native to the lips of Pancho Villa, and so this bold and terrible man, full of ambivalences and contradictions, delighted with children and fond of slitting throats, sang out ecstatically the melting strains of romantic Mexico.

No wonder María Luz Corral succumbed, no wonder she married the man! Pancho seemed so different from the rest of her suitors. This one called her *güera* and *chula,* his pretty little blonde. With any of the others she would have become a typical housewife; with Pancho the path promised to be strange and wicked. She chose the strange and wicked. He was her eternal lover —so rough but oh, so gentle. They were married on October 17, 1909, in the small town of San Andrés, near Chihuahua City, the bride's family and a few friends being present. The ceremony went briefly and smoothly, without interruption. But at the back of Pancho's head one thought repeated itself, the *rurales* might hear of the wedding and attempt to capture him during its ritual. If they chased him that day, they were far, far behind—perhaps misdirected while in hot pursuit by some *compañero* stationed at the crossroads as a lookout for any such emergency. The wedding being duly consummated, the pair of lovers must have been very happy in being finally united, considering the many separations they had endured during Villa's sojourns in the mountains. Among the slanderous reports about Villa, none ever attested that he so much as once ceased to love María Luz Corral. She was his first sweetheart, and, of his many wives, the only one he loved until his death.

Love among the other bandits partook only of animality. The outlaw breed turned to the stewing brothels, *los serallos,* while Villa, the gay *caballero,* sought real romance, which dwelled elsewhere, in another, better part of town. The outlaws, foul and smelly, were a band of men unloved and unlovable, stupidly salacious, unskilled at courtship, who had to buy love from the professionals. With jingling coins bulging their pockets, they constituted the life-blood of vice, the backbone of its economy.

Some of them broke their pattern when, in a wild act, they convulsed a country girl with early wisdom of the sexual secret. They purchased her silence with *dinero,* their healing cure and cheering anodyne. Theirs was the vicious custom of a pre-revolutionary day.

Only the women of the *cantinas* truly welcomed them, these rough and tumble *hombres* who strode into the *bailes,* restless and drunk and wicked. They pulsed with purpose at the gaming table, swore loud at the crowded bar, grew purple with lust while they danced. When a pretty new *señorita* entered the room, she dashed to its center, and in it danced a solo. As round and round she swept, other girls joined her, each in her turn dancing similarly before the circle of men. Bored with gambling, taut with *tequila,* the bandits lighted into flame caught from the *baile,* argued and shoved and stumbled, with shameless oaths and lascivious leers.

Probably on these occasions, to enlist the sympathy of the dancing women, the bandits rang out one of their lonely songs. If Villa joined them, as sometimes he did, he sang the mournful chant, too.

I have three vices
And I have them very badly:
Drunkard, gambler, lover.

The outlaws attained celebrity at the *bordellos*. Even the non-professional women seldom refused them when they put every question into the melody of song:

If I drink wine
And ask credit of no one,
If I get drunk,
It is because I have money.
What am I going to do
If your love is what I want?

Stories about the gay *caballero* abound along the border. In Parral, Pancho once met a young woman by the name of Petra Espinosa, whom he raped when he could obtain her in no other way. He lived with her carnally, and she bore him several children. In Mexico City he took a fancy to a French waitress who nearly died of fright when he boldly approached her with a rough proposal of "marriage." At this stage in the Revolution (1914) officers and men, flourishing their guns about, brazenly chose any woman they liked. The waitress had reached the point of hysteria when the French *charge d'affaires* rescued her and somehow explained to the impetuous Villa that romance proceeded less ferociously in France.

A similar episode features Pancho and an American blonde, a *turista* from El Paso who liked to flirt with men. The big blonde accustomed herself to visiting the Juárez bars. When the drinks began to tell on her, she courted anybody she saw. Apparently the flirting never went beyond the harmless stage, but the handsome *bandido* who then gazed at her, with curling lips, did not know this. For a night or two he courted her at a distance and gave her the "eye" by placing his right finger below his right eye and pulling the eye wide open—a sign meaning "I have my eye on you." The blonde blanched at the sign and turned yet whiter when somebody told her that the *caballero* bore the name of "bloody Villa." After that, she restricted her drinking to the bars of El Paso.

A rather amusing anecdote has for its setting the El Dorado Bar in Juárez, where one evening he began talking with the owner, Jesus Valdez, when Villa suddenly spied an attractive little barmaid who did not recognize him to be the famous *guerrilla*. First, he gave her his provocative "eye" sign; next, he rubbed his doubled right fist against the right side of his face, a gesture in the lingo of the netherworld, meaning, among other things, "let's get going." Then he leaned across the bar to speak with her.

"Little Flower of the El Dorado," Villa said to her, "you are by far the loveliest barmaid in all Juárez. I, Pancho Villa, wish that you would sit with me as I drink."

The bold *caballero* smiled and pressed her arm to lead her to his table, but the girl would not go. She gave him a negative gesture of her own, thrusting her right hand toward him with the three middle fingers folded and with thumb and little finger extended and turning in a tilting movement, to mean, "Nix, you tell the little white lies." Then the diminutive barmaid stood straight up and spoke in her lilting sing-song.

"Señor," she said, "I do not know you. But this I know, you are not Pancho Villa, who this day fights the army at Sercanza. The news of this fiery battle reached me just now. You—you of the drooping mustache and forward manner, if you be Pancho Villa, then I, Lucia Calderon, am the Empress Carlotta. I do not like your manner. You should well remember that Villa has the charm of a gentleman and does not pass the time in small, dark bars. He lives in the sun, fights clean battles, and makes short work of little men like you."

This crushed Pancho the philanderer. Crestfallen, he hurriedly strode from the floor, stumbling through the dark swinging doors of the El Dorado into the night.

Pancho made his most unheroic appearance in the vengeance he wreaked upon a woman who had borne him a son in the little town of Santa Rosalita. After a lapse of some years, Villa, returning there, discovered that during the interval of his absence his *señora,* María Amelia Baca de Villa, had married a new husband with whom she lived happily. Pancho calmly ordered his men to execute the husband. Then he coolly escorted the mother and child to a stake and burned them. As the flames engulfed the pitiful forms, no expression whatsoever showed upon the face of Pancho Villa—no pity, no remorse, no anger. The natives claimed afterwards that when the fire died down, gray ashes piled up. From amid these protruded plainly a human finger, the round and stubby forefinger of a child pointing upward to Heaven.

Villa, in some tales, turned into a beast: he tied a father to a chair while he assaulted his daughter before his very eyes; he gave his perfumed nude girls, sleeping companions of the night, to his men every morning for

community playthings. A more gruesome fate befell
Pablo Avila and his beautiful wife, Rita, owners, in
1910, of a prosperous pawnshop in Juárez. One night he
and two of his drunken soldiers entered their pawnshop.
After plundering the place, one of the besotted men
pointed a gun at Pablo Avila's head while his heated
companion assaulted the pretty matron, Rita. The
couple were helpless, and that night the brutal band
made sport of their agony. The next day they stationed
Pablo Avila against a wall, peppering him with shot until his blood and brains bespattered the ground. Then
the executioner Villa, the refinement of whose cruelty
surpassed that of the Spanish aristocrats whom he hated,
commanded the weeping Rita to take a broom and sweep
up the brains and dump them in a can. This the hysteri-
cal woman did. The horror of these experiences, they
say, drove her insane. A week afterwards she died, of
shock and a broken heart.

In most of the tales Pancho was pictured roman-
tically as a rough but gay lover. Although he could act
the part of a monster, usually he behaved as a warm
and human fellow—a somewhat emotional type devoted,
according to the legend, to the search for an ideal
woman. He oddly insisted, in view of his own infidelity,
that his sweethearts be faithful to him. The more he
philandered himself, the more he longed for a mistress
loyal and true.

He won lasting celebrity, too, as a troubadour. Villa
developed into a good mixer with convivial groups; he
merely sipped at his beer, but he sang enthusiastically
with his *compañeros*. He excelled at singing ranch songs
still popular in Mexico and the Southwest. His soldiers
taught him the words, but he learned the tunes naturally,

having a good ear for a lively *canción*. He liked to hear
his favorite tunes being played on the piano, being quite
proud of the pretty one-step, *"Tierra Blanca,"* composed
in honor of one of his victories. When moved by music,
Villa exuded happiness and became a jolly fellow. His
mind relaxed as he caught the spirit of the tune while
dancing with a sultry *señorita* who held him close.

To women, Pancho Villa possessed a quality both be-
witching and *triste. Sí,* they knew he was married, even
sympathized with his separation from his beloved. But
mainly they thought of his sadness when he lived without women off in the mountains. Pancho would sometimes depict himself in a pitiful plight, would beg the
pretty *señorita* to remain faithful until his return. One
of the songs they sang in those days, entitled *"El Aban-
donado,"* told of the loneliness and sorrow of the abandoned Villa and his outcast men.

> You abandoned me, woman,
> Because I am very poor,
> And because I have the
> Misfortune of being married.
> Well, what am I going to do
> If I am the abandoned one?
> You abandoned me, woman,
> *Adios, adios.*

If the bandits lodged in a small town, they courted
the country girls. They invented adventures about their
experiences in Mexico City. Better still, they chanted
the verses of *"La pajarilla"* and promised the girls, little
birds in a gilded cage, trinkets and baubles, clothes and
perfumes, all the gaudy merchandise of the city.

When you go to Mexico, Rosita,
You'll probably go through the streets
    singing:
"I am, gentlemen, a bird in a cage.
Who of you will go with me?"

These simple folk ditties rather accurately portrayed the man Villa. After all, in the Mexico in which he lived —with the populace upset by war and rumors of revolution—the women welcomed the opportunity to share their love with the romantic outcasts. In this way they escaped their own tension, the tedium of their endless days. Trite as it appeared, the portrait of Pancho the lover contained only one picture, a man in the likeness of a romantic *caballero* who regarded *amor* lightly, who accepted it carelessly wherever it offered itself, who took it as naturally as he did meat and drink. Pancho Villa never attained the stature of a Don Juan, but neither did he sink to the dimension of a modern bluebeard. He grew into a lusty fat Mexican who liked the women, and the women adored him in return. He would do the right things to please them, simple and not always expensive things, like singing them a song, putting a shining pearl necklace about their necks, or emptying a pocket of his gold into their laps.

Throughout his life Pancho's heart warmed at the thought of *amor,* and he befriended other lovers, helped pining sweethearts who found themselves in distress. With a smile wreathing his face Pancho Villa encouraged his men to take women. Meanwhile he set them an example. Pancho the passionate! Fat, *sí,* but indefatigable, and *muy, muy simpático!*

Pancho once aided a young *señor* named Gabriel. The youngster chanced to be losing his sweetheart be-

cause her father, Don Samuel Granados, bitterly opposed their marriage. The father's chief objection rested
on the belief that Gabriel had insufficient funds to provide a comfortable living for his daughter. Pancho,
whom the young Gabriel had once befriended, heard of
the difficulties of the two lovers and determined to do
something about it. The outlaw chieftain knew that a
wealthy banker, Don Simon, who lived in the town of
Santa Maria del Oro, had a large sum on hand in readi-
ness to pay off the miners who worked in that district.

With his merry men, Tomás Urbina, Juan Salas, and
a third bandit called El Mocho Eugenio, Pancho ransacked the bank safes and left the building an empty
wooden hulk. Then he warned Don Simon that he would
kill him if he divulged the identity of the robber. The
next morning the bandit chief visited Don Samuel Granados and his beautiful daughter. Upon arrival, he first
met the pretty *señorita*. He told her that he was Gabriel's
friend, that he had come as his agent to see her father
about asking for her hand in marriage to his *amigo*. The
girl asked the visitor his name, to which he reportedly
answered : "My name is José Mendosa."

The girl introduced Villa to the father, after which
she retired. Don Samuel still objected to the match after
being offered a substantial sum of money, whereupon the
so-called José Mendosa declared his real name, swearing that unless the father consented to the honorable proposal, he, Pancho Villa, would take his daughter to
Gabriel at once. The alternative hardly sounded pleas-
ant, and the old man hurriedly accepted the marriage
arrangements engineered by the outlaw. The couple
were happily wedded and remained eternally grateful
to Villa. When a son blessed the happy pair eight years
later, they remembered him and christened the child

Francisco, calling him "Pancho" for short. The bandit's fame as a benefactor spread so widely during pre-revolutionary days that *peon* mothers often named their sons after him.

A lot of the time, satiated as he must have been, Pancho grew tired of women. On these occasions real excitement proved necessary to heat him up. Gunfire, the smell of gunpowder, must have broken his thermostat and let his passion rise. In a fancy *cantina* one of his lieutenants gave a Federal officer's girl a wide, libidinous eye. The Federalist resented it. As the lieutenant continued to wink as well as make signs, making audaciously evident his intention to make off with the long, lissome girl, the officer suddenly drew his gun and shot the lieutenant in the mouth. By the time the dead man pitched forward, Villa had fired from under his left arm and drilled the Federalist officer cleanly through his forehead. Instantly he grabbed the girl and dragged her away to make love to her. Yes, it must have been the sight of blood that turned the fat rooster Pancho into an insane, volcanic gamecock.

What was his *pasion más grande?* It was the celebrated love of Villa for a beautiful courtesan of Durango, a woman who in the end gave up her life for him. The tempestuous affair of Pancho and Adelita became the most tragic romance of the Revolution.

In a private dwelling in Parral a ravishingly beautiful young woman stood at twilight before her mirror, putting the final fluttering touches to her already perfect toilet. Her perfume smelled faint and peppery, but it endured, hanging in the air like an unseen but odorous red carnation. Dark olive, of tall and elegant stature, she was the embodiment of Mexican beauty, her full proportions being such as to awaken the desire of Villa, who favored the robust type of woman. This fragrant *seño-rita* had great dark eyes and beautiful raven hair, the coils of which a rich yellow scarf bound lightly. Her soft skin kindled into flame at the caress of a masculine hand. Beneath a silken yellow blouse, there rose the firm, proud, rounded breasts of a ripening young woman. At twenty this wild animal of a girl looked like a goddess, a *fiera del amor*. Already betrothed to the blond Portillo, one of Villa's loyal men, she hated to surrender her freedom without one last fling. The servants who attended her quailed before her radiance. They complimented her profusely as she pivoted on her tiny high heels before the looking glass. She was a dangerous, a terrifying, young woman, this Adelita—one who had a longing for mad adventure. The serving women, veering about her, kept up a shallow flow of chatter.

"I could almost believe you were making a conquest of General Villa tonight," a wise old *tía* finally said.

"Who knows, my aunt," Adelita replied coquettishly. "Look at me, *tía,* and tell me, do you think the General will find the famous Adelita of Durango too homely?"

At the banquet hours afterwards Adelita made a speech in honor of Pancho Villa. Throughout her talk, which ended with the expressed hope that he would become the president of the Republic, she cast her hot eyes on him.

Villa's first reaction prompted him to make an ironic comment: "This little pug-nosed cutie also thinks I long to become president."

But after being presented to her, Pancho talked alone with her in a nearby garden, surrounded by *olmos* and *zapote* trees. This time he did not make impetuous love; instead, he gazed into her volcanic eyes and told her rapidly, in an impulsive self-revelation, the torrid story of his vengeful, fevered dreams. He had won glory as a man of quick action, on the battlefield or in the hour of love, and at the last he embraced Adelita, kissing her not unwilling lips with an open, hungry mouth. Meanwhile, a melancholy but amorous song aided his suit— *"La cantela,"* from the Bajio region of Michoacan— which a group of brightly-clad *"Dorados"* entuned in the dark distance.

> I find myself a prisoner by cunning,
> I find myself imprisoned by a woman.
> As long as I live in the world and don't die,
> Never in my life will I love again.

> It wasn't the truth
> That she promised me.
> Everything was a falsehood.
> False was the money she paid me.

> We took for granted that we were trash.
> Along came the whirlwind and took us up;
> And while high up in the air we flew,
> The same wind blew us apart.

Suddenly a man's head peeped around a nearby *zapote* tree. Portillo, Adelita's betrothed, stepped into the garden just as Pancho Villa finished kissing Adelita. Villa stood there with his mouth wide open. Portillo paused, evidently torn between rage and despair; then, with a hopeless gesture, he pushed his gun into his own mouth and thunderously blew off the top of his head.

Villa, who had not known of Adelita's betrothal, could hardly believe his eyes as he, petrified with surprise, gazed uncomprehendingly upon the scene. Portillo had been a favorite *compadre* of his. They had been like brothers. After discovering the truth, he swung around bitterly toward Adelita, roughly shook her by the arm, and commanded his men to get rid of her. When he spoke, he trembled with surprise, anger, and deep grief.

"Get this woman out of here; take her somewhere, anywhere, so long as I never see her again."

The blond Portillo, the friend of Pancho, they buried in a special tomb with a pair of his grief-stricken leader's best boots beside the grave. These happenings Villa never forgot. One night a year or more afterwards, Villa grew sad with memories of the past incident. He tracked down his favorite singer, a Mexican named Ochoa, requesting him to sing something new to soothe his nerves. Then Ochoa sang, for the first time, the mournful verses of *"Adelita."*

> Adelita is the name of the young one
> Whom I love and cannot forget.
> In the world I have a rose
> And with time, I shall pluck her.
>
> If Adelita should be my wife,
> If Adelita should be my woman,
> I would buy her a silken dress
> So I could take her to the barracks dance.

On and on Ochoa sang, through ten more stanzas of *"Adelita,"* until sadness overcame Villa. He walked aside, to a place apart from the fireside, bowing his kinky head and weeping his hard bandit tears. *Triste,* the memory of love was *muy triste,* ever so hard for a bandit to bear.

Pancho Villa's unlucky encounter with Adelita had an aftermath. Destiny allowed him to see her again, to behold once more her smoldering face, but nevermore in tempestuous love. Unknown to General Villa, she dressed herself to join his army as one of his *"Dorados,"* his "golden" bodyguards. One afternoon during the bloody carnage of battle, the General observed a youthful *"Dorado"* who wore upon his neck a silken yellow scarf with a blood-red center. After the slaughter, the incident stuck in his mind, bothering him as he walked among the corpses to count his losses. With consternation he spotted the yellow bandana with its red center, for he had ordered his *"Dorados"* to remain out of the fight. Here lay one, however, who had lost his life by disobeying his orders. Villa received the most crippling impression of his life when he discovered the corpse to be that of Adelita. The girl had died heroically, fighting for her General like one of his bravest soldiers. Villa leaned over the maimed, torn body. Emotion so overcame him that he only murmured : "She was a *Dorado, a Dorado."* Later on, in fond recollection and as a token of gratitude, he built a tomb for Adelita. He built it in Parral next to that of her blond sweetheart, Portillo. Years later, when he was inured to suffering, the strains of *"Adelita"* always brought to his face a dolorous shadow; he then had the haunted look of an *hombre muy triste.*

In the final picture of the amorous Pancho there appeared a lover neither malicious nor cruel to either his wives or his mistresses—if they remained faithful. He derived happiness from women, perhaps a kind of inspiration. People often alleged that he had only one weakness, an inordinate passion for the *señoritas,* but this was hardly so. Pancho enjoyed the pagan trinity, wine, women, and song. He smoked and drank sparingly, but he paid time-and-a-half service to both love and music. Villa heard the sirens call, if anybody ever did;

he answered them, warmly, with the melting melodies of Mexico. *Las mariposas de la noche* consumed much of his time, more of his money, yet they paid him a priceless return. In their company he relaxed, became a different man. Relieved of tension, of memories of the blood upon his hands, he thrilled at the sight of a smoldering female, pouring out his pent-up heartaches in gorgeous song. His technique originated in carelessness, not in force: the novelty of his absolute lack of seriousness overpowered the naïve, startled maids. But the man who played thus at love had one day to rue his gaiety. He thought that happiness came from word and woman and way; and that the word was tenderness, the woman love, and the way—Where, indeed, was the way?

Stung anew with grief, Pancho sensed to his marrow that the way had been with the sultry Adelita. The more women he loved these latter days, the more insistently he desired for them to be faithful. He who had been so unfaithful himself came now to doubt the existence of loyalty in others. He demanded what he himself did not give. Only much later did he rightly appreciate the love of his maturity, the devotion of María Luz Corral. Pancho paid the penalty of the gay *caballero*. As he grew older, he realized that in his prime he had known too many sweethearts. Now he suffered from a surfeit of what had once pleased him most. Tragedy had its hour upon the stage in his tremendous drama of human love.

In the midst of his gaiety he breathed anew the pungency of spring apple blossoms which was the perfume of María Luz Corral and recalled how little he deserved her fidelity. Where now were all the *muñequitas lindas,* those little *loco* dolls, he had known and loved? Sweet little Cuca, of Juárez, flower of the Rio Bravo, with her wonderful, wonderful scent of attar of roses? Tall Petra, pomegranate of Delicias, who was so passionate, so taut, tense, and madly tigerish? These days a lump came in his throat when he saw a bedraggled juvenile girl, once of the country and now of the city, go by singing her contrite song of *"La pajarilla"*:

> You already know that I am a caged bird,
> One who once happily ran through the forest
> Enjoying the spring
> And the perfect songs of the birds.

Or when laughter cascaded everywhere, he called to mind the vanished beauty of the dead Adelita, buried now in the rock-fenced countryside of Parral. At times when he heard the mocking notes of *"Adelita,"* Pancho Villa sensed a strange trouble deep inside: once, in a fleeting moment of humility, he even lit a candle in *la iglesia.* His bandit heart did not break; but he stirred inside with an odd kind of resentment.

> Do not cry, my beloved woman;
> Do not be ungrateful to me;
> Do not make me suffer so much.

"Güera," a word applied to a woman with a light complexion, was the pet name Villa called his pretty wife, María Luz Corral—one of many proofs that he loved her deeply. For her, he built, in Chihuahua City, a beautiful home known throughout Mexico by the name he gave it, *"La Quinta Luz."* After his death, one of his three wives, Señora Estroberta Rentería, laid claim to some of his property, but the Obregon government decided in favor of María Luz Corral de Villa. She provided a home for a number of his children born

from other women; she, in various ways, displayed a warm and forgiving nature. Though his enemies said that Pancho once sought to divorce his wife, such behavior may well be doubted. Señora Villa is the best witness on this point. In her volume, *Pancho Villa en la Intimidad* (1948), she portrayed the human side of her husband's character: fortune-hunting women, she said, chased her husband, not *vice versa;* and then she added: "I was the only woman that Pancho really loved."

All of that happened long, long ago. In those days sometimes a full picture came into focus, that of the sad lover of dead Adelita, of the devoted husband of Luz Corral. . . . Then the portrait dimmed. There followed sound and action, plenty of both. Thundering hooves heralded a raid! The air burst wide open with wild yells, *"Viva Villa! Viva Villa!"*

In some hungry town the champion of the poor succored the needy. That night there was food aplenty; that night a young *señorita* in her garish room, the soft light of a blue lantern pulsating above the bed, yielded her body to him for gifts, fingering her trinkets as he made love, turning on her arm a bright bracelet, round and round. Later, much later, Pancho Villa threw her aside. From a wandering singer he heard the first strains of *"Adelita"* drifting in from the street—and quickly, *muy pronto,* Villa's mood began to change. A throbbing memory convulsed him with hopeless longing, achingly.

When he gazed outside, the light from a swinging blue lantern in a *tambor* came and went. Pancho, a young and yet decrepit red rooster, his comb crumpled and drooped, felt old, old and dejected. He suffered not from age but from overindulgence. No wonder he had difficulty in crowing these days.

"Qui-qui-ri-quí," he quavered—once.

CHAPTER 6

Gold of the Sierra Madre

Along with Pancho's love for women and song, there grew an equal, if not greater, passion for gold. His lust for treasure had its roots in his abounding sex drive: he could not have his women, his Adelitas, Petras, and Cucas, without gold to heap in their laps until their heads were agog with amazement. Gold and women at the start formed inseparable complements in his bandit lift. In time, the greed for money began to outgrow the original demand of necessity, the golden wand whereby he entranced his women. Finally, avarice threatened to become a vitiating force in his character.

He had other vital stimuli besides women in his quest for the magic metal, and these constituted a saving grace for him. He rewarded with bountiful shares of his plunder the faithful *compañeros* Lopez, Trillo, and Urbina until each of them became, in his own right, a rich, a powerful, man. When he met poor wayfarers upon the rustic roads or woodland trails, he bought food for them, greasing their constantly itching palms with *pesos.* To the *peones,* it appeared clear that no man, not even the incredible Pancho Villa, could have so much money as he flaunted about unless, of course, he knew the secret of the Sierra Madre.

Pancho Villa first became interested in mining at the age of nineteen. Having decided to quit the hidden life, to mend his thieving ways, he took up peaceful residence in Hidalgo del Parral, a small city in Chihuahua noted for its vast resources in minerals and ore. In this Parral he met the simple farmer, Pedro Alvarado, a namesake of the Spanish Conquistador. Now Pedro had little acquaintance with gold; had seldom, if ever, dreamed that good fortune would really someday catch up with him. Pancho Villa and Pedro Alvarado worked together on a small farm near Parral, turning up the gray soil and digging out the clay-covered boulders which they kicked aside in order not to obstruct the growth of the green shoots they planted in the fertile earth. The men talked as they labored, using the strange make-believe language of rustic Mexico. Theirs was an inimitable speech, an adult mode of expression which had, within its composition, a strong flavor of the naïvete of children. The Mexicans at peace with the world and themselves, as these two men were, became mellow, lazy, half-asleep.

"Why is the earth so low near that little tree, Pedro?" Villa asked.

"It is *nada,*" Pedro replied. "You make a poor farmer, Pancho Villa. The afternoon passes; you must dig the earth, not talk about it."

"*Sí,* Pedro, *yo lo sé.* But still a man wonders. The rain it does not wash away the soil beneath a tree. Look at the big trees. The earth is high about their trunks. Their branches and leaves keep the soil dry beneath them; their soil does not wash away."

At this juncture Pedro Alvarado gazed about him, because he could never be as interested in his work as he pretended; and, besides, he liked to wonder, too, about

that little tree. Their life on the farm went so peacefully
that except for their musings about nature, they could
never have passed the daylight hours away. As Pancho
said, it was odd about the little tree, for, look! how low
and shallow the soil stood at its base. Maybe that was
why it appeared not as full grown as the taller ones sur-
rounding it. Pedro Alvarado took pride in his earth,
with its animals, its hills, its foliage. Overcome with
emotion, the farmer began to sing *"La higuera,"* but his
song of the fig grove failed to distract the busy Pancho,
who continued to dig deeper and deeper.

> The fig grove is dried up
> Because the roots were exposed.
> My love doesn't love me any more
> Because I am on a drunk.

> Oh, what high and hilly steeps,
> How they are tossed by the winds.
> He who doesn't believe it
> May go and return in the afternoon.

> *Venderemos el toro y la vaca;*
> *Venderemos la becerra;*
> *Todito venderemos, mi vida,*
> *Todito, menos la tierra.*

> We shall sell the bull and cow;
> We shall sell the calf;
> We shall sell everything, my love,
> Everything, except the land.

Then Pancho suddenly cried out, *"Mira, Pedro, aquella palmilla!"* as he pointed toward the little palm tree, to the humble and dreamless farmer, for his pick had struck a vein of ore.

Since the property belonged to Alvarado and the discovery of the lode to Villa, the lucky men became equal partners. For years they shared together the opulence which came to them through the successful operation of the mine celebrated as "The Little Tree." Some of the later knowledge of the mining industry displayed by Pancho derived from his earlier experiences with *"La palmilla."*

The ultimate fate of this gold mine became enshrouded in the mists of tradition. Perhaps it was not gold at all that Pancho found but a treasure of great value, a large collection of jewels and doubloons which some fearful Spanish miser had hidden away in the earth for safekeeping. Whether it was a gold mine or, as the later tale goes, a buried Spanish treasure, must not have mattered much to Pancho. What happened to the partner, Pedro Alvarado? Here, too, the plain answer is that nobody ever heard what went with him after their gold "strike."

As for Villa, he went back to the bandit breed, and with his old *compañeros* returned to the northern state of Chihuahua, to its high hills and gay cities. A song about his departure, *"Me voy,"* echoed the abandon with which Villa, now stocked with gold, flung himself into his saddle, turning his horse's head toward romance in the far northern border country which ends at Ciudad Juárez, home town of his recent "flame," the maddening Cuca.

I go to the hills, *guiri, quiri, quiri;*
There waits my girl in Ciudad Juárez. . . .
I go to see the girl of my love
To contemplate her lovely countenance.

Always Pancho Villa had to hide his gold, so that he would have it to spend upon his good-looking "butterflies," his *mariposas de la noche.* In Chihuahua, the beautiful capital of Chihuahua state, Pancho and his staunch men once, supposedly, buried a huge chest of valuables. The treasure was hidden somewhere near the dam at Chihuahua, during Revolutionary days—just after Rodolfo Fierro, Villa's "Butcherer," executed Tomás Urbina at Pancho's command. That Villa had to get rid of Urbina proved a tragedy. Yet Villa was not the first leader to be betrayed by a former friend. Urbina had recently been hoarding his treasures gained through looting and plundering, but he had not been dividing the spoils, as in the prescribed manner, with Villa and his other *compañeros.* Villa had always taken care of his men and given them a share of the loot. Urbina, in his deceit, had deserted Villa to operate on his own. They had to chase the man to capture him, and in the exchange of gunfire Urbina received a wound in one arm. Villa promptly asked him about the money and jewelry he had brought from the state of San Luis Potosí. Urbina replied that he had no money to speak of and no jewels.

"If I had the money and jewels they accuse me of," he explained to Villa, "I would have split it with you long ago."

Pancho did not believe him and said: "Split, you dirty traitor," before he directed his men to search for the loot.

Under the ground, below the back room of the house in which Villa conferred with Urbina, the searchers quickly discovered the huge loot that had been stowed away. The amount which they found consisted of over one million *pesos* worth of expensive jewelry and about one million *pesos* in solid gold pieces of ten and twenty-*peso* denomination. The cache unearthed was tremendous, representing the total sum of Urbina's wealth, which came largely from the bank robberies he had made in the state of San Luis Potosí. This comprised the hoard which Villa's men took back to Chihuahua City with them to hide safely away in a hole dug in the ground near the dam. After his experience with Urbina, who was guilty of treason in neglecting to bring reinforcements to the battle of Celaya as he had been ordered to do, Villa hardened noticeably, becoming a thoroughly skeptical and embittered man.

When it came time for Urbina to pay for his mistake, Villa offered to shoot it out with him. The *cuento* asserts that Urbina refused to choose one of the pistols, thinking that Pancho might then forgive him. Instead, Rodolfo Fierro strung him up, tightening one end of a rope about his neck before he put him on his horse standing there beside him. Then the bandits, two or three of them, tied the other end of the rope to a limb of a cottonwood tree and drew the rope tight. Just as Urbina turned about to say something, Villa threw a rock and hit the horse's rump. The *caballo* jumped high and forward; the head of Tomás Urbina for a while spun round and round on the rope.

Pancho Villa was not "bad." His experiences with men and gold drove steadily home one lesson to him, the fact that he could not trust anyone to look after the proper division of the spoils except himself. Thereafter, Villa acted with unusual care to see that nobody shared his innermost secrets. He took particular pains to see that no one except himself knew for certain where he hid his gold—his gold, that of Parra, and anybody else's he could lay hands on.

It was in the little town of Zaragosa, not far from Ciudad Juárez, that Villa left another *entierro*. After one of the Revolutionary battles at Juárez, Villa rode away with one chest and two men at evening and returned at dawn empty-handed and unaccompanied. Although Villa was a close-mouthed *hombre,* he made a slip of the tongue that day about his buried treasure chest. Two loiterers, Pedro and Jesús, overheard him.

The sound of the word *oro* quickly excited the blood of these two adventuresome Mexicans, who immediately set out for Zaragosa to look for Pancho's chest of gold. That night in Juárez they loaded their horses with picks and shovels, cantering quietly toward Zaragosa, so that their *compañeros* would not see them leaving, or learn of their route. Pedro knew that Villa cached the treasure trove in the ground on the outskirts of Zaragosa, near a heap of boulders, and that the place was marked by stones piled together to form a cross. They reached Zaragosa without mishap, soon thereafter spotting a rocky section of terrain in the outlying country.

"Mira! There is a cross," Jesús suddenly exclaimed to Pedro, for there in the gathering twilight loomed two crossed columns of white rocks that looked exactly like a cross.

The two Mexicans began to dig at once with their picks and shovels. The noise of their work grew so loud that one driver on the well-traveled road nearby slowed his car down when he passed them. Becoming frightened that others might discover their good fortune, they stopped digging, deciding that they would begin afresh early in the morning before the citizens of Zaragosa were astir. The early part of the night they talked about how lucky they had been to locate the exact spot where the cross was; the later part they slept some distance away near their saddles and horses and dreamed of castles in Spain, of the moldy old chest that would be packed to its top with fat gold doubloons.

The next morning Jesús awoke Pedro when he screamed: *"Donde está la cruz, la cruz?"* The two men gazed at the blank rock pile a little distance off with terror and dismay, because the cross had disappeared.

Almost out of their minds, Pedro and Jesús stayed at Zaragosa all that day. They dug and dug and shovelled away, but to no avail. The cross had vanished, and without it as a landmark they could do nothing except wear themselves out moving boulders and pitting the earth with shallow holes. They never were able to find the treasure, either at this time or in later undertakings. If the cross could be relocated, the gold would be easy to excavate. The chest could not be buried deep because it was large and difficult to handle. Once a poor laborer walking near the Rio Grande picked up, on a particularly rocky spot of earth, a scabbard and the crown of an old *sombrero,* probably a part of the belongings of one of the two companions Villa killed to safeguard the secret of his hiding place.

It is known, in support of the gold stories, that Villa had much knowledge of the Rio Grande. He not only roamed its southern banks but crossed to the northern side. *Paseños* tell of when he visited El Paso and of how he came to hide his treasure near their city. He visited Madero there at the outbreak of the Rebellion, and in the next year he met Captain Juan Hart and saw more of the country. With Captain Hart and other friends, he went, in 1911, to Cloudcroft, New Mexico, a village among the clouds. During a longer sojourn in El Paso, in 1913, he displayed a lot of money, a fact to remember about his hiding gold, and spent it freely. His credit rated high then, because he won a reputation for paying his debts. He bought all kinds of arms and supplies to keep his armies in good condition, always paying the cost of whatever he purchased in raw gold, of which he seemed to have an unending supply. He bought expensive clothing for his wife, Luz, and his brother, Hipolito. Wild about automobiles, Villa bought his wife a new Hudson, a de-luxe sedan, and a Cadillac for himself. Soon tiring of the Cadillac, he gave it to Hipolito and got himself a Dodge, which he found easier to manipulate.

Before returning to Mexico, he decided to do something about his money, the protection of which was worrying him a lot. He could not trust it to a Texas bank, which might go broke. Naturally he then thought of the heights of the great Mount Franklin, above El Paso. Reared as a mountaineer, he had already explored its fascinating recesses. One day, about twilight, he came upon a marvelous spot for hiding his trunks of gold safely from the sight of mankind. As soon as he had tested the location from every angle, to make certain that it was as secure as it looked, he climbed down the slope to get his car. It proved much easier to hide gold in Texas than in Mexico, where he always felt harried as though watched by a thousand eyes. A thousand eyes!

After he buried the trunks in the rocky earth, Mount Franklin loomed like a great "Mother" *sierra* herself, with all the many lines of electric illuminations below, in the border cities of El Paso and Juárez, glowing as brightly as a necklace of pearls about her throat. Today they share the secret only with Mount Franklin and the Rio Grande flowing silently at its feet.

When Villa went back to his Mexican home, he became active in the Revolution anew. Again he started spending money at an ever increasing rate. To get it, he taught his army to loot the towns that favored the Federals, and so his men ransacked their buildings for whatever they might contain in the form of valuables, art relics, or money from tax assessments. The mining industry had long been familiar to Villa, and soon he began to put *"la mordida"* on the *gringos* who owned mines in Mexico. "The bite" became his regular practice. By 1915, when he rode the tide of political supremacy, he had confiscated all foreign-owned mining companies. His male bosom must have swelled with unusual patriotism when he made inventory of his rich British and American holdings. From these sources, he gathered literally millions of dollars in silver and gold. He stole so much of the stuff that he hardly looked at the ore to see what it was. This carelessness once caused him embarrassment. When he unloaded some money bags to pay off his men, they discovered that the pieces were, not silver, but lead soft enough for them to bite with their teeth. But every other time it proved to be the real thing. Soon he was faced with the problem of disposing of a new fortune.

Pulpito Pass lies between Sonora and Chihuahua, off west from the Sierra Madre, of Durango. It is a tall,

tight, tortuous canyon; and somewhere within it Villa
hid his new treasure, stowing it away in wheat sacks.
While his companions went on a trip to Chihuahua, he
remained at camp with fourteen mules and ten Indians.
When his men returned four days later, they found Pancho all saddled and packed and ready to move on.
Quickly they noticed something else. There were the
fourteen mules, all right, but where were the ten Indians
and the heavy sacks of "wheat" that had clinked like
metal when hauled into Villa's rooms? During their absence Villa had packed the money on the mules and
taken the Indians along to help him bury it. As was his
custom, he brought back only the mules!

And this could be, for one fact is certain. When Villa
lay imprisoned at Mexico City in 1912, a signed confession was extracted from him. He said that he did not
want to be called a *"ladron"* and denied that he had any
large holdings. He did say, however, that he once had
buried money in the earth and admitted that in a certain
place *"en la sierra de Santa Barbara"* which he could
not *"identificar por una descripción"* he had buried five
thousand silver *pesos*.

In one of the tales Pancho Villa selected a rather
fantastic place for hiding his loot. Once a man identified
only as Señor Franco, who was moving from Mexico
into Texas, brought along his household properties, including a brass bed with detachable knobs on its four
hollow posts. Its original owners, friends of Villa, had
sold it to Señor Franco before he came to El Paso. Nobody at the Customs detected anything unnatural about
the bed in the examination. Now, it happened that the
Francos had a small, blind son who always stayed at
home, playing with his toys and with the brass knobs on

the bed. Frequently he loosened the knobs, so that the parents constantly had to screw them tight again. One day the boy managed to get the knobs off and to dig his fingers into the posts, which brimmed with solid gold pieces packed so tightly that they had not rattled when brought across the International Bridge. Being blind, the youngster did not recognize the coins for their worth and scattered them over the bed and about the floor. Late that afternoon, when his parents came to wake him from his nap, they were startled to see hillocks of gold heaped everywhere. They thanked God for their good fortune. The grateful parents then took the boy to a famous eye specialist in Chicago, where he regained his sight completely.

Villa later spent a great deal of his money on a farm at Parral. He made it into an estate, a breathtaking showplace of the Republic. In doing so he found it necessary to unearth some of his hidden loot. Once, prior to building a new mill, he and his friends, Trillo and Elias Torres, went to Santa Cecilia, where, years before, he had left gold hidden in a house. When they reached the place, they found the same old pecan trees growing there; but the house was in bad condition because its walls had fallen down. Villa went to what evidently had been the fireplace, where a small depression showed in front of it.

"I believe that somebody has beat me to the money, because of the dip in the earth. But look, dig here," Pancho said to one of his laborers, "and do it carefully, *poco a poco.*"

Everyone stood back while the digging occurred. They waited expectantly; no one spoke. Suddenly the pick hit something. Then Villa took the shovel and dug out the earth with great care, so as not to hurt anything. Then the shovel hit the top of a box. Everyone heard the muffled thud.

"Clean these sides," Villa said to a laborer, "and take out the box carefully."

A decayed old box came out that looked like a wooden case for holding wine bottles. It brimmed to overflowing with gold pieces covered with mud and blue mold, and some of the *dinero* fell out of the box when it was lifted from the hole.

"This is one of my treasures," Villa said. "Now we have enough to buy that mill for Canutillo."

Although Villa continued to be remarkably successful at hoarding fortunes which he stole from others, he was, in one respect, like the proverbial fisherman: he let the biggest one get away! Luis Terrazas, a Spanish don celebrated for his art treasures, his magnificent carriages drawn by white mules, and his luxurious *Quintas Carolinas* built for his children, held the title of the richest cattleman in Mexico. His favorite son, Juan Terrazas, had buried the mass of their fortune somewhere near his home in Chihuahua City. At least Villa's men thought so, and one day the outlaw band invaded Juan's house. In order to show Juan Terrazas that they meant business, they drove their sweating horses right into the front living room, letting them trample on the opulent furniture and excrete their dung over the richly carpeted floors. They shooed the wife and children into the backyard, where they strung up Juan Terrazas to a tree. Villa was everywhere notorious as a torturer. He had maimed men up and down the length and breadth of Mexico with the "Mark of Villa"—a clipped ear, a missing nose, a disfigured face, a crippled foot. He and his "gang" had become devils. They got sport out of tying an enemy behind a wagon to be dragged in the dirt and horse manure. They liked even better tying the arms of a man to one horse and his legs to another, so that the plunging animals pulled the fellow apart. On this occasion they tied Juan up by his thumbs, torturing him while they repeated one question: *"Dondé está el oro?"* Incredible as it sounds, Juan endured the worst they could do to him and did not reply. Villa's men took time about whipping the aloof Spaniard with their quirts, but he fainted from the pain without telling them his secret. The Terrazas, aristocrats to the core, were as strong and proud as the *peones* who opposed them. Juan kept his secret; and Pancho Villa lost that treasure, a fabulous *entierro* of great prize.

In another story, Villa once sent two of his *Dorados* to meet a certain General Limón and deliver to him $100,000 in gold. The messengers never arrived, so General Limón rode off into the Maniquipa Canyon, of Chihuahua, to locate them. About the middle of the canyon he found four dead men, the two *Dorados* and two American soldiers, but no trace of the gold. Since Apaches lived there, a young brave had found and buried it. But he soon went away to college in Mexico City and did not reappear until long afterwards. People then queried him about the gold, but he proved unable to answer. Each time he started to talk, evil spirits sent him into fits. These finally maddened him and left him too frightened to do or say a thing.

The richest treasure in the world lies today untouched somewhere in dark fastnesses of the Sierra Madre. Villa had been careless about caching his *oro* during the Revolution, when he had no leisure to locate it safely. Upon retiring, in 1920, he brought together the fortune he had scattered far and wide. With the aid of forty workmen he hid it in the Sierra Madre. Embedded in a cave, or a series of caves, piles upon piles of gold and silver bars, sacks of gold and silver coins, little chests of sparkling rubies and diamonds remain where Villa left them. Some gold hunters have estimated its worth at one million dollars, while others believe it to be of fabulous value. In some ghostly underground cavern of the bewitched mountains, from whose recesses the bats and the "witches" fly at night, there rests, undisturbed, Villa's lost fortune. The secret of its lodging place has gone to the grave with the man who accumulated it, Pancho Villa, and with the workmen whom he supposedly killed after they and their burros had hauled the treasure to its last hiding spot, those marked men whom he selected for a journey without return. The men were buried in graves which they dug for themselves before Villa shot them down, watching the bodies fall into their self-prepared tombs. Only the bats know the secret now, the bats and the *"brujas."*

The community burial place of the forty men who helped Villa haul the loot was found afterwards in a locale far removed from the eerie peaks of the Sierra Madre, but the skeletons in the tombs revealed nothing. Someday the "witches" may tell a lonely fugitive or a poor woodchopper what happened during those long hours that Villa and his workmen hauled the fabulous cache into a secret underground passage not so many years ago. They had to make many trips to stow it all away. The treasure is thus certainly there. During the night the *"brujas"* fly far to the north, as far away as the silvery Rio Grande; at dawn they return to their resting place amid both silver and gold in the cavernous bowels of the Sierra Madre and chuckle over the secret which they and the bats share only with the dead. It is the money of dead men and much blood is on it.

The *leyenda* of Villa's treasure in the Sierra Madre is persistent. The reports of the *entierro* stress the fact that the forty men who accompanied Villa were Indians native to the Barranca del Cobre and that they sufficiently eluded his vigilant eye to leave a number of provocative hieroglyphics, or strange Indian signs, on a few of the rock ledges scattered among the tall *piños* trees and forested areas of the upper regions of the mountains. The signs were made with *burro* blood, for the native workmen cut the tendons of one of the pack mules, using the blood to paint and scrawl their strange markings. In dry seasons the signs can hardly be seen, much less deciphered; but when wet with the rains, or when water is poured on the rocks, the donkey blood comes to life again and turns blood red. Aye—bloody as the *oro* for which perhaps ten times forty men forfeited their lives to Villa's passion for the precious metal. These crimson petroglyphs are symbolic of the treasure which they may some day disclose: a dead man's treasure whose resting place is guarded by the eternal silence of dead lips.

The *mozo,* Miguel Sanchez, who enjoyed his leader's confidence, could have divulged the location after Villa's death, but he did not. For some reason, Villa trusted Sanchez and did not kill him as he did the workmen. He became so friendly with this *mozo* that they drove about together over the country in Pancho's Dodge automobile. Miguel Sanchez knew the correct route to the buried loot, for he was there. Unfortunately his death, in 1925, removed the last person who knew the exact whereabouts of Villa's *entierro de oro*.

What marvelous secrets must be stored away in the Barranca del Cobre, of the Sierra Madre—held close to her bosom in the rocky caverns within her ghostly forest tops. The silent Tarahumare Indians, celebrated throughout Mexico as runners, have gone to the Canyon of Copper and brought back one or two rare nuggets of greenish gold. Prospectors visiting in this wild terrain of weird deserts and flowering *olmos* trees have been put to flight by nomadic bands of roving Mexicans—remnants of Villa's original band. Other "gold bugs," like a group of men students from the University of New Mexico in 1952, carried geiger counters which registered strongly on the earphones, but they returned empty-handed. More recently, a gambler from Nevada won a map to Villa's cache from a drunken *peon* in Juárez. He took it home with him to Las Vegas, where he intended to hire some gunmen to return with him as "prospectors." Perhaps he will come back and locate the gold, for Mexico is a country full of mysteries.

The green waters in the streams of the Barranca del Cobre derive their color from copper mineral deposits and, in the spring, are fed by swelling rivulets from the heights behind them. As the rivulets rush down the mountain gorges, they carry with them occasional nuggets of *oro* to be deposited in the valleys below. Whence come these nuggets, no man knows. But in the heart of the Sierra Madre the water is a deeper, darker green than anywhere else and the gold shines with a braver, brighter lustre.

VILLA AT THE BATTLE OF OJINAGA

VILLA AND LUZ

VILLA THE OFFICER

VILLA AT JUAREZ RACE TRACK

1. Col. Matt Winn (Kentucky Derby promoter)
2. Gen. Villa
3. Gen. Hugh L. Scott (United States Army)
4. Major Mickie (on staff of Gen. Scott)
5. Gen. Rodolfo Fierro (Villa's "trigger man")

CHAPTER 7

Scourge of Chihuahua

By 1900, young Señor Pancho Villa had grown to the stalwart stature of a defender of the poor and oppressed. To some extent, he utilized his kindness to the needy as an excuse for his gory escapades; but he and his *compañeros* came, after a while, to believe that they stole cattle and killed men in behalf of a "Cause." For ten or more years he literally waged war against the *hacendados*. The punishments which he had received at their hands, as well as the disappointment he experienced when none of them would hire him after his term in jail, rankled in him strongly. Little by little he increased the range of his forays. Somewhere near, he knew, there existed plenty of silver and gold. Soon he broke the monotony of his continual raids on the *rancheros* by a newer venture, beginning to despoil the properties of rich *gringo* mine owners.

Before the Revolution, Villa raided both the American Smelting and Refining Company and El Potosí Mining Company, two large corporations with headquarters in the city of Chihuahua. At a later date, after he had become a leader in the Rebellion, he attacked in other places of the Republic. Once, when raiding the Cusi Mine, he ordered a miner to be shot. The man, dressed in a well-tailored suit, acted unruly: Villa commanded him to remove his suit and give it to a ragged soldier; the condemned miner became enraged and threw the coat in Villa's face. Pancho so admired this show of bravery that he set the miner free and later made him a captain in his army. This act revealed the Villa of the heart.

His black ferocity showed itself a year afterwards in his massacre of the Chinese at Chihuahua City. Had China not been a weak country, her government unquestionably would have intervened and probably declared war on Mexico. Villa despised all Chinese, so much so that if he wished to insult a white American he addressed him, contemptuously, as a *Chino blanco*. It was Villa's men who conducted the brutal, animalistic slaughter of the helpless Chinese. The yellow men almost never put their money in the bank, either from ignorance or through fear it could not be reclaimed. The custom with them was to keep the money in their pockets or hidden elsewhere on their persons. The hasty thieves turned loose all their pent-up ferocity upon the unarmed Chinese, and simply to facilitate rifling their clothes, the Villistas shot them down as soon as they saw them, never pausing to ask if they carried money. The outrage amounted to more than a slaughtering of the yellow race. It became a cowardly massacre of a defenseless minority wholly innocent of any wrongdoing. Such an infamy could only have happened during a sanguinary revolution by a rabble of brutal fellows already marked as outcasts and villains.

Precisely how guilty was Pancho in the annihilation of the Chinese? Although he avoided the spotlight when this villainy was afoot, his guilt went deep. Never a man to be caught "red-handed," he choose to be the master mind and had his band to do the dirty work.

Mr. Duncan Jones, who, for twenty-five years, worked as a lumberman in Mexico, encountered these Chinese-hating Villistas in 1915. While he resided in Pearson, General Martin López, second in command to Villa, stormed into town with four hundred mounted and well-armed men and seventy-five extra horses. The spare horses General López brought along to carry off the loot. He first raided the general store, making its owner give them what they wanted. In return, the General handed the owner a signed receipt for the goods. Mr. Jones said that when he last heard of him the owner still had that receipt. When night came, the soldiers continued riding up and down the streets. Along about seven-thirty, two men rode hurriedly up to Mr. Jones and jumped off their horses onto the unlighted porch of his house, where he lived with two other Americans and a Chinese cook. The first thing they asked was why he had no light: *"Porque no hay luz?"* So he turned on the lights and inquired what they wanted. They asked if he had any Chinese: *"Tienes Chinos?"* He said "No," thinking that his Chinese cook had gone, since the Mexicans had killed seven of them that day. When they queried him, they poked a gun in his stomach and began to search his pockets.

"The Villistas," Mr. Jones continued, "took my silver dollars and asked me for my watch, which ticked away where I had it fastened under my underclothes. I ∕as expecting to be robbed, but they didn't hear it ticking and so missed the watch. Then they started searching the rooms for a certain kind of blanket and found none to suit them. They came to my room, threw the cover back and the mattress to see who was under the bed, jerked their guns out, and said, *'Quién está abajo de la cama?'* As I had a fine blanket under the bed, I told them it was a blanket. They said: *'No; es hombre.'* I looked under the bed and there was Joe, the Chinaman. I said, 'Come out, Joe.' They put a gun to his temple, but did not pull the trigger. They relieved Joe of seventeen dollars and a watch and asked me why I had lied about the Chinaman's not being there. I explained to them that we thought he had gone and showed them the lunch we had fixed for him to carry with him. I could understand more Spanish then than I could before or since, and so I understood them when they gave us orders to have the Chinaman cook their supper and said that in thirty minutes they would return with the Colonel with them.

"When they got back, they asked about the Chinaman. We told them that he was so scared he turned 'white' and left. We were cooking supper for them ourselves, and while they were eating, the Colonel gave me three dollars to pay for the supper, and I handed the three dollars back to the Colonel and told him he was welcome to the supper. And that's the biggest lie I ever told, for I hoped the food would petrify them.

"The next morning the private soldiers began to come up and wonder what we charged for meals. I told them, 'Nothing,' and to come on in and we'd feed them, as I thought it a good policy to stand in with the soldiers. Later in the morning the Colonel returned for breakfast, and after we fed him, I asked him to stop the privates from coming because we were getting short on vittles, but we didn't mind feeding him. I also told him that they robbed us last night. The robbers were the two men who

came with the Colonel to supper, but he said he didn't
know it. He let out a cuss word and said, 'Why didn't you
tell me and I would have killed the *cabrones?*' Then he
said, 'We're leaving this afternoon and going over to Colonia Juárez, a Mormon Colony.' I heard later that there
they robbed a flour mill, that they even took the rings off
of women's fingers. Later they went on to Ascención, and
General Martin López was wounded in a battle and died
later from that wound."

On the very day of López's raid, Mr. Clarence
Cooper, owner of a saw mill in Pearson and a close
friend of Mr. Jones, was conferring with Pancho Villa
in Casas Grandes. Fearing their town would be attacked, Mr. Cooper had gone to Casas Grandes to ask
the *jefe* to leave them alone. On his arrival he found
Villa fast asleep. When he woke up, Villa at first said
nothing but stared at Mr. Cooper as he talked. Finally
Villa interrupted him to say that he would have killed
him if he had acted afraid but that he liked the kind of
American Mr. Cooper was. Then he said that since Mr.
Cooper had once helped the wife of one of his generals
he would take care of Mr. Cooper's enemies if he had
any. He also promised not to go through Pearson. The
town, of course, was, nonetheless, raided. This incident
demonstrated again that Villa, while avoiding a personal appearance himself, permitted his officers to do
about as they pleased.

The Villistas rampaged on such a large scale that
nearly everybody, be he rancher or lumberman, American or Chinese, lived in fear of their approach. Miners,
in particular, feared their raids. During the Revolution,
Villa took all the reserves of coal which he came across
in order to keep his army moving by train. He caused the

mining industry to quit operations on more than one occasion by stealing their fuel. If he had no need of it, he
traded the coal for American supplies in El Paso. He
had special ties with the American Smelting and Refining Company. When its plant was abandoned, he seized
the machinery and briefly tried to use it with the forced
aid of native workers. When payday came, he was without funds and offered to pay the natives with slices of
lead bullion. He may have been deceived by the bluish
metal, which shone and looked like silver, but the workers were not. They promptly refused to accept the lead
as payment for their labors.

From his encounters with *gringo* miners, he derived
a queer knowledge of the English language. Like any
other foreigner, he learned the words which he heard
Americans speak most frequently. When a *gringo* asked
him if he spoke English, he replied, *"Sí;* American
Smelting *y* son of a bitch." The fame of his snappy retort
spread to the length and breadth of Mexico. Villa's reactions were unpredictable. During a friendly agreement with the *gringo* miners whereby he hauled bullion
on his trains in exchange for their coal, he again used
English. They asked why he associated with the Ameri·
can Smelting Company and he said, jocosely: "I am pro-
tecting the smelter from bandits."

Ordinarily the American mine owners tendered Villa
"protection money," which he usually took but once ig-
nored. In 1915, Mr. Edward Plumb, an employee of El
Potosí Company, in Chihuahua City, kept hidden in his
room about $50,000 in gold, a sum then owed Pancho for
"protection." The bandit, however, never asked him for
the money and gave him a passport of "safe conduct" in
northern Mexico.

On the other hand, three years later, Pancho was incensed with the Americans for turning from him to Carranza. About October, 1918, he kidnapped Frank Knotts near Villa Ahumada, where Knotts operated the Erupción Mining Company. He held the American for a ransom of $20,000. The captured miner's brother, Mr. A. W. Knotts, of El Paso, brought the bandit the money in a large wad of bills. But Villa refused to accept the bills because he said that he hated the faces of the *gringos* stamped upon them and demanded that the ransom be paid in gold. It took a while to satisfy this new demand, but, at last, on November 18, Frank Knotts regained his freedom, he and his friends celebrating the happy event a few nights later with a banquet at the Paso del Norte Hotel.

The relations of Pancho Villa with the Mormons were likewise both friendly and strained. Once he captured a Mormon woman and forced her to accompany him and his men on their raids. When she won her release, American officials asked her about the treatment which she received. She replied that they treated her with all the dignity due a woman and had not molested her in any way. At other times he behaved less chivalrously. He once raided the home of a young Mormon mother in Colonia Dublan and confiscated all the food, money, and clothing. Busy with stealing, he turned to the pretty mother to remark: "You wait, *señora*. I will sleep with you tonight." The Mormon woman, terrified by this prospect, waited until he became preoccupied with his looting and then quietly slipped out the back door. She ran as fast as she could to the home of a *peon* family nearby, where there slept a newborn infant. She told her Mexican neighbor about the threat, and that

Señora dressed her in a *serape* so that she looked like a native. Then she took the baby in her arms and pretended to nurse it. Villa grew furious when he discovered the lovely Mormon had eluded him. He charged about the place for thirty minutes before going on to pillage another quarter of the colony. In his search, he peered in at the door of the *peon* house but failed to recognize the young mother and her feeding child as the woman who had escaped his clutches.

The Mormons had reason to fear him, at least when he suffered from his murderous rages. One time they lit huge fires outside one of their cities to mislead him into believing that it was being destroyed and therefore not worth attacking. Again, just before the battle of Torreón, they allowed him to take their wagons for use in this battle. The Mormon owners accompanied Villa in the vain hope of being able to salvage their wagons but neither carried arms nor fired upon the enemy. Beyond this, his association with the Mormons did not go. As they were prosperous, it was remarkable that he let them off so easily.

Villa was often prone to behave in an unexpected manner. A distorted sense of humor came natural to him, as when he purposely left proof around that he alone deserved responsibility for a crime. In those days there existed a popular American phrase, "I.O.U.," which Mexicans quickly picked up from *gringo* tourists. Pancho Villa soon learned to use it, too. When he stole American cattle, say three hundred head, what he left their owner was his "personal card," a piece of rough paper boldly scrawled—"I. O. U. 300 head. Pancho Villa."

Another indication of Villa's twisted humor comes

from a story about his blind burro. Living then in Chihuahua, he needed a better mule to bring home special supplies from Juárez. When he stopped at Guadalupe, he met a *peon* farmer there and tried to swap him his blind *burro* for a strong mule. The *peon* refused to trade and walked away into his fields. As soon as he vanished from sight, Pancho substituted his *burro* for a young animal he found in its stall. That night the tired farmer found out what had happened and grew angry. He told everybody in the neighborhood how Villa had tricked him and run off with his best mule. About a week passed before Villa came through Guadalupe again on his return trip. The *peon* and his children were then in the fields and did not see him stop by their house to put a package inside the front door. When they returned home at nightfall, they were surprised to find that Pancho had left a big bag of money to pay for the mule he had taken the week before.

The theme of Villa's epic recurred whenever he aided the humble. One time he met an aged man who chanced to be losing his ranch, and asked him about the mortgage. *El viejo* told him that in recent months he had grown too decrepit to work and had been unable to meet the payments. When Villa asked him the amount, he said that he owed two thousand *pesos* and would never be able to earn that much *dinero*. Villa then jerked a roll of bills from his pocket and counted out two thousand *pesos* into the grateful *peon's* hand.

Villa got much money, which he generously handed around, from the attacks he continually made upon the large feudal estates of Don Luis Terrazas. These estates reached so far that it required more than a day for a horseman to ride beyond their limits. Like Texas, in the

United States, Chihuahua is the largest state in the Republic of Mexico, and nobody could traverse it in any direction without crossing land which belonged to Terrazas. Before Villa depleted his herds, he had the name of one of the richest cattlemen in the world. He lived like a proud Spanish don, a *grandee* who became famous enough through his own efforts to be duly elected governor of Chihuahua. The number of his beeves, prized in both Mexico and the United States, grew to legendary proportions. When a Chicago firm ordered a million head of his cattle, Don Luis's reply by telegram was said to consist of a brief question: "What color?"

Pancho vented his hatred for the Spanish nobility upon far-ranging droves of the cattle of Terrazas. Being free from anything except his whims, he operated on his own irregular schedule and never struck in the same place twice. Terrazas, unable to anticipate when or where his next raid would come, failed repeatedly to ambush him. Since Villa had a large band of outlaws, Terrazas, at the last, avoided meeting him in open conflict; for when he did he lost his workmen as well as his cattle. A Spaniard who had fought victoriously against the French in Mexico and whom President Benito Juárez had rewarded by giving him a ranch empire, Don Luis Terrazas stayed helpless in the struggle with Villa. All of his military knowledge went for naught against Pancho, whose mad *banda* rode helter-skelter into his herds, firing their pistols this way and that, careless of limb and property, contemptuous of human life.

Much like a sullen mountain cat, Villa pounced upon the big droves of cattle. He stole the fat beeves to stock the farm of a *compadre,* to provide meat for a starving *peon* family, or to sell in his own butcher shop in Chihuahua. He killed off the *becerros* by the thousands. In slack intervals Pancho the Puma waited with cunning, exultant in his primal strength, until at last hunger devoured him. His brown eyes then turned yellow as he thought of the tall, thin Spanish *grandee* who, except for him, ruled as "Lord of Chihuahua." Year after year he slashed away at the ripe herds. Intermittently, by day and by night, he struck on the unpredictable schedule of a creature of the wilds. He cut and stabbed at the *becerros* until they dwindled, until Terrazas was a ruined and broken man, while Villa, an animal creature, fattened and gloated in the hills. Friends of Don Luis report that just before his death, he swore that his spirit would appear before God on the Day of Judgment to denounce his enemy as "Villa the Villain."

The verdict on Villa—what should it be? He hated Don Luis Terrazas. As a *peon* struggling to rise above his caste, he loosed his blind anger on him as the summation of all the evils of Mexican feudalism. To him, Don Luis was a miser who paid his broken *peones* twenty-five *centavos* per day, who ruled a boundless region but made his landless poor sleep in hovels, who let his hopeless slaves stagnate in ignorance. From this man more than from Don Arturo López Negrete, he conceived a hatred for Spaniards that became a ruling passion of his life. Villa, while a bandit, did not organize the *peones* into an armed front against their oppressors, but he ignited them with some of the fire of his own dangerous fighting temper.

A prime cause for his success with the masses was that they did not look upon him as a real thief. In those days the numberless droves of Mexican cattle were everywhere regarded as the unbranded beeves of a free territory. When this vast public domain was autocratically deeded to Terrazas by the Federal government, simple people like Villa saw no justice in such an arbitrary transaction. One of his men, Lieutenant Colonel Ybarra, explained the matter succinctly: "After Pancho Villa moved to Chihuahua, he came upon a great amount of free or loose cattle. Nobody owned them. They were not branded. Pancho and his gang would round them up and sell them to rich cattlemen and ranchers in Texas." The attitude of Pancho himself was well expressed in his own words to his friend Elias Torres: "What do you think, Señor Torres? Do you think that I should regard the animals born in the wild as belonging to Terrazas when he did not know of their existence nor take care of them? My little brothers and I had the same right to the wild creatures as Terrazas. Do you think it was only the right of the old rich men to brand them and call them their property?"

After Villa prospered, he did not forget his *peon* origin. Promptly he brought into his *banda* the outcasts, the fugitives, and the helpless. He gave refuge to frightened *hombres* whose masters had beaten them unmercifully, violated their homes, and debauched their daughters. To many of these, he gave the new freedom of his mad, carefree life. He planted the seeds of revolution in the *peon* mind, and his onslaughts upon the ruling class sprouted them. Since he burned with a love for the masses, he flaunted his robberies recklessly before the world.

The day their little daughter died Señora María Luz Corral sent messengers to her husband, Pancho Villa, with word of the child's death. These messengers, so the story goes, were detained and mistreated by Don Luis

Terrazas and his men. When he at last heard of his bereavement, Pancho became enraged with Terrazas. He had the blood lust when he rode towards Chihuahua that night and swept through Terrazas territory with vengeful, blazing guns. In a mad fury he and his bandits fired at everybody they saw. Next day the *rancho* of Don Luis was a shamble of ruins.

Quickly, before anybody knew it, Pancho had taken over the land, beat Terrazas, and won the idolatry of the *peones*. With the maker of a *corrido,* each of them took up the cry that

> What my country needs
> Is Señor Francisco Villa!

In Villa, the scourge of Chihuahua, the long-suffering *peones* had a leader, a brawling *hombre* who could transform their cry into action and make its meaning clear. A pugnacious patriot stood ready, now, to carve history out of a bloody revolt.

CHAPTER 8

La Oportunidad

To Pancho Villa, the Revolution provided the opportunity to make his countrymen forget his dark past while he strutted, before their eyes and those of the world, in the guise of a patriot. Everything turned out almost exactly as he wished. People north as well as south of the Rio Grande despised the Díaz regime. In El Paso, a cannon, located in the Plaza, was donated to the rebel cause. Numerous El Pasoans supported the Rebellion by donating money, ammunition, and moral support.

Pancho the Opportunist joined the rebels in 1910 through Don Abran Gonzales, a fiery revolutionist, who had the title of provisional governor of the state of Chihuahua. Well liked by the Mexicans, many of whom quickly identified themselves with his political stand, Gonzales set about raising a citizen army. About the time he made his last will and testament in El Paso and returned to Chihuahua, there to form insurgent forces for skirmishes against the towns of Gomez Palacio, Madera, and Parral, he received a messenger from Pancho Villa. Villa now offered the services of his entire outlaw band to the Revolution. Gonzales accepted the proposal with enthusiasm, immediately dispatching the following reply to the *bandido:* "I appoint you, by the authority

vested in me, a Captain in the Revolutionary army."
Villa saw clearly what he stood to gain by joining the
fight. Hitherto he had skulked in the hills; now this
skulker, as big as life, strode plainly into the open, ready
to run rampant throughout the length and breadth of
Mexico. It happened as though fate itself had con-
spired on his side to give him this chance to whitewash
his bandit character. A golden opportunity glowed before him; he plunged headlong to grasp it.

December 10, 1910—the date he reported to Gonzales in Chihuahua City—became a milestone in the career
of Captain Francisco Villa. Pancho, about twenty-two
years of age, led, not his complete forces, but only forty
of his best fighters. Governor Gonzales talked rather
seriously with him, saying: "Society has made you what
you are. I know you hate Díaz and all he stands for. Now
is your chance to fight on the side of right. We want to
liberate the enslaved masses of our country. We want
equality, a democracy like the *Americanos* have. . . ."
The conversation had no strong effects on Pancho then.
He knew what he fought for without having somebody
tell him: he fought for personal profit. Later on, he
learned to feel much different and became enamored of
the rebel cause.

His first assignment was to report to General Pascual
Orozco, Commander of the Revolutionary Forces. He
and his forty new volunteers, on arriving at the camp
near Casas Grandes, made a poor impression, and
Orozco conceived an instinctive dislike for the unkempt
group. Like a "gray champion" of old, Villa, coming
straight from the wildwood to the rescue of his country
in the hour of its distress, looked the part of the humble
hero and nothing else. He reported in his "work" garb—

a *charro* outfit with boots, spurs, and a black bandana momentarily at rest beneath his pugnacious chin. Envy entered into Orozco's attitude toward the raw recruits, for Pancho then cut a considerable figure as a bandit. Only yesterday, off in the Sierra Madre, he had been the Puma of the Pines, grinning all over his face and licking his fat chops. Now his appearance among Orozco's troops from Chihuahua created an uproar, as the person of Villa in buckskin provoked envy.

The proneness to envy, a shortcoming of the leaders of the Revolution, characterized both Orozco and Villa. The rebel Pancho, until his death, remained beside himself with enthusiasm and ambition. Accustomed as he grew to the worship of his robber band, he despised knuckling in to Orozco. Crippled by a deaf ear to either authority or good advice, as shown later by the way he spurned the words of caution delivered by his friend, Felipe Ángeles, before the crucial battle of Celaya, he instinctively hated his new commander. He said afterwards: "In General Orozco's eyes all I could see was treachery."

Yet Pancho gained one thing from Orozco. Through him he met Madero, the amazing man who fomented the Rebellion.

Don Pancho Madero—that is, Francisco Indalecio Madero—almost single-handedly started the Revolution. He became the idol of Pancho Villa. He became so, even though they derived from two different worlds. Pancho was a *peon;* Madero, an aristocrat. Pancho was uneducated; Madero was a man of learning. Villa was unreligious; Madero, devout. The only common ground of the two patriots was their love of country. The vegetarian Madero, black-bearded and hollow-eyed, looked like a visionary. In him heart, dream, and mind combined to make a spirit more potent than brute strength. Known as "The Little Fellow," he held the physical as nothing. His slight frame housed a soul that alternated between diffidence and audacity. In battle he remained far too undecided to give the order of attack. Characteristically he postponed, deliberated, and changed his strategy a thousand times. Yet he could look forward, could lose sight of physical injury to his own person, could forget himself in a cause. And he could talk. Since 1908, he had talked on the street corners of Mexico City his rambling, contradictory talk. As a vegetarian, he asked the populace not to kill animals; as an aristocrat whose family had become impoverished, he urged the same populace to overthrow the government then in power. When *guayule,* a raw source of rubber, was discovered growing in abundance on his family property, Madero knew it meant his cue to act, since he now had plenty of money to carry his vision into practical reality.

One day this mystifying little vegetarian, later the owner of a twelve-cylinder Thomas Flyer touring car, perambulated into the presidential chambers, confronting the aged Porfirio Díaz, the enemy of *peones* and Yaqui Indians, who had tyrannically ruled Mexico for thirty years. Brazenly, black-whiskered Madero asked white-bearded Díaz to resign his office. The startled Díaz stood aghast, beginning to sense that he was drowning in the fiery, audacious eloquence of the spiritualist. Madero—called "The Redeemer"—behaved like a man entranced, his fanatical eyes burning with inward rapture. With the spellbinding magic of his strange words he delineated before the eyes of Díaz an outline of the Utopian future of Mexico. Don Francisco Indalecio

Madero produced a thing metaphysical—a word picture of a democratic tomorrow for the Republic. Díaz became flabbergasted by this prophet who acted like a personage from another world. It never occurred to him, bowed by age, weakened by illness, and conquered as he was by the memory of his own inhumanity, to quench the overpowering flow of rhetoric by having Madero jailed or shot. Instead, the sick old tyrant hearkened to the diviner. Díaz, half persuaded, asked who could bring these wonders to pass. Madero said: "I could."

He could and he did. In sleepy San Antonio, Texas, on October 10, 1910, Madero proclaimed President Díaz as a dictator who had defiled his office. A month later he declared himself "Provisional" President of Mexico. It happened then that "Madero the Spiritualist" brought his vision, his personality, and his message to the thriving border city of El Paso, where the Mexican populace, together with a sprinkling of Texans and other adventurers, became ignited with fervor for the "Cause." *"Viva la Revolución!"* echoed up and down the borders of the Rio Grande, the impoverished but hard-working *peones* improvising a short song in honor of Madero as their liberator.

> *Mucho trabajo,*
> *Poco dinero;*
> *No hay frijoles!*
> *Viva Madero!*

How did the relatively unheralded Villa, then known merely in the northwestern states, come to the attention of a great national leader like Madero? At the outset of the Revolution, Pancho occupied a minor position in the revolt before suddenly sweeping into prominence. Outside of his native Durango and neighboring Chihuahua, Pancho had only a name, and a rather bad one at that. He had not nearly so much celebrity as many of Madero's other partisans— positively not so much as General Orozco, whose orders he had to accept, obey, and carry out. Pancho possessed an irrepressible, volcanic spirit. In a matter of hours after his induction in the army, the one and only Pancho drew the full glare of the spotlight to train itself on his now portly but fierce figure and on one of his illegal but humorous actions.

On his first night at the army camp, Pancho stole a beautiful white horse from a nearby *ranchero*. Of course, he already had his azure Appaloosa as well as a pony or two, but he could never conquer his weakness for horse-flesh. Now that he was a Captain, he thought it but fitting to add another horse to his *remuda*. Before dawn, while in route to Casas Grandes, he had spotted a magnificent Arabian stallion and had determined to "steal" him when night fell. Not "steal" exactly, for again he thought of the theft as a levy, as *la mordida*. . . . Should not the *rancheros* be glad to contribute a horse, or anything else, to see that they were properly protected, and by a captain too? It was the same old Pancho, all right. Horses and women remained his first weaknesses. and, after that, murder. Everybody knew it, for everybody living in Chihuahua has always claimed some kind of "intimacy" with Pancho, being either related to him, or to somebody personally shot by him. But this time he had to oppose a general, one who grew livid with rage. As soon as the horse stealing became known, Orozco publicly bawled him out, angrily placing him under arrest. The Pancho whom the *peones* called "Savior and

Defender of the Poor" first entered upon the stage of the Revolution as Captain Villa the Horse Thief. Clearly an army could not be molded with bandits like Pancho around. For the sake of morale as well as to teach the need for loyalty and obedience, Orozco decided to make an example of the horse thief the next day by having him shot at sundown.

Fortunately for Pancho's health, Lieutenant Raoul Madero, brother to the national leader, succeeded in interceding for him with the General, saving the bandit's life. Some people said that he telegraphed Francisco Madero for a reprieve. Pancho, who spent a sleepless night pacing up and down his *adobe* cell, was virtually trying on the well-knotted noose for size when the reprieve providentially arrived, and he was duly released. Meanwhile, Orozco, crestfallen, hid his disappointment, biding a more propitious hour to conquer the strutting rooster, Villa.

The struggle for Casas Grandes, which led in turn to the first battle of Juárez, began the next day in earnest, with the arrival of Madero at the head of his troops. Villa's friend, Lieutenant Colonel Ybarra, said: "Francisco Madero, a candidate for president, was looking for backers of his candidacy in the Chihuahua *sierras* between Juárez and Chihuahua City. After Villa's group joined Madero's troops, they had a battle with the Federalists, Porfirio Díaz's men. The Federalists were organized and consequently defeated the Maderistas at San Andres and Cerro Prieto. The citizens then declared themselves Maderistas and immediately joined the troops and, little by little, forced themselves to the border until finally, in Casas Grandes, Chihuahua, the Maderistas defeated the Federalists. From there they proceeded to Juárez, where they defeated the troops led by Juan J. Navarro. Villa and Obregon wanted Madero to assassinate Navarro. But Madero being an illustrious and honest man forgave Navarro and deported him to El Paso. With the taking of Juárez by the Madero troops, the great unrest of the Federalists died, and General Porfirio Díaz left Mexico for Europe."

At the battle of Juárez, Madero's ragged, refractory army of about 2,500 was led by a "menagerie" of international warriors: Captain Oscar O. Creighton, an American nicknamed "The Dynamite Devil"; Captain Sam Dreben, an American touted as "The Fighting Jew"; Lou Charpentier, a Frenchman known for his operation of cannons; Colonel Guiseppi Garibaldi, Italian descendant of the grand liberator; Colonel Eduardo Hay, an American partisan; Tom Mix, an El Pasoan who later became a famous actor; General Pascual Orozco, champion mule-packer of the state of Chihuahua; Captain Tracy Richardson, an American adventurer fresh from conquests in South America; General B. J. Viljoen, a celebrated South African fighter; and, of course, Pancho Villa. These adventurers composed a muster roll difficult to match anywhere.

Paseño sympathizers on the Texas side of the river included women nurses, who volunteered their services in a provisional hospital then established in El Paso. One nurse, Miss Juana Napoles, met the Maderista, Pancho Villa. She saw him as a "nice-looking, fair-skinned and blue-eyed man." In her account, "Villa was the idol of the poor people. It's true he plundered and robbed the wealthy, but he was a humanitarian and distributed the loot to the poor. People would line up in long queues and he would give them money and food."

In this first battle of Juárez, Villa distinguished himself as a fighter, overcoming the bellicose Felix Mestas, owner of a saloon on Noche Triste Street and partisan of the Federalists. Several years later, enemies of the Revolution invented the yarn that Mestas was a harmless civilian whom Villa tortured without mercy. However this was, it cannot be denied that innocent parties suffered. Shells fell on the Texas side, five El Pasoans being killed and fifteen wounded. Those favoring Pancho, among the Mexicans, spoke glowingly of his bravery, stretching small incidents into gargantuan feats. The *peones* said that during the fracas he laughingly caught the cannon balls of his enemies and threw them back down the big barrels of their guns. As soon as the firing ceased, the *peones* paraded about, exaggerating their own doings and investing their *jefe* with supernormal accomplishments. The Revolution made important history, which supplied, as always, the source for oral tales and folksongs. A modern miracle actually occurred in this year 1911, when Hector Worden, an American in Madero's Constitutional Army, took to the air. This was probably the first aviator in the world to participate in armed hostilities. Later on, in 1913, Villa himself hired a group of famous *gringo* pilots, largely from Chicago, such daredevils as Mayes, Farnum Fish, Rhinehart, Mickey McGuire, Wild Bill Heath, and Klaus Bergenthal. Thus fact was again at the basis of the *corridos,* one of which enthusiastically exclaimed:

> Pancho Villa no longer rides a horse,
> And neither will his people;
> Pancho Villa owns an airplane,
> And he gets them with great ease.

This first battle of Juárez, which lasted two days (May 9 and 10, 1911), forced Díaz to flee to France, whereas Francisco Madero, in Mexico City, became the new president of the Republic. For a breathwhile all seemed peaceful. Pancho, who had risen from captain to colonel, returned to Chihuahua City. But, in March of 1912, Orozco broke with President Madero, launching a fight to overthrow the new government. Instantly Pancho struck a blow to the south in favor of the Maderistas by defeating, on April 6, the Orozco sympathizers at Parral. He directed the people of Parral to take twelve carloads of food stranded on the railroads, so that they turned to him fanatically. In the meantime, Emilio Vasquez Gómez, at Juárez on May 6, proclaimed himself *"Presidente de la Republica."* Some days afterwards, when Maderistas beat his troops just outside Juárez, Gómez sped rapidly to El Paso, to be heard of no more.

Learning this, Villa, who had started to the rescue of Juárez with a thousand men, proceeded, on May 18, to Mexico City for a visit with President Madero. Madero, however, ordered him to return to Jiménez to join forces with General Victoriano Huerta in the contest against the rebelling Orozco. Pancho disliked subservience to a superior officer and now, as once before, got into trouble. Maybe he stole another horse, or perhaps a woman; maybe he committed the unpardonable act of stealing Huerta's *tequila,* for that general was overly fond of his *copitas.* The strongest likelihood is that Huerta, secretly hating the rebels and merely pretending to favor Madero, simply wanted to remove Villa from the scene of action. On some kind of trumped-up charge, horse-stealing or the like, he sentenced the ex-bandit to the penitentiary in Mexico City and dispatched him there by rail under heavy guard. Curiously, Madero had faith in Huerta and did not intervene.

No one, in fact, came to his rescue. He had volunteered as a "friend" of the Revolution—he then held the rank of Colonel—but now he languished in a cell as a degraded convict. Month followed month as he sought friends and endeavored to plan a "prison-break." Finally on Independence Day (September 16, 1912) he escaped with an accomplice. After four months of imprisonment, he at last made his way as "Doroteo Arango" to a hotel in El Paso.

Villa's hideout at Second and El Paso Streets hardly ranked among the spine-tingling scenes of his turbulent career. He was a refugee or, worse still, an escaped prisoner. Living in a section of the city known as "Little Chihuahua," he momentarily plumbed the depths of frustration. Though without political friends, he wanted to regain the favor of the Maderistas by murdering the traitor, Pascual Orozco. The Maderistas, however, frowned on this suggestion, so that he frittered away the time at the hotel, rarely having any other visitor in his room than the accomplice he had brought with him. His friend, Otto Schuster, eventually ferreted him out in the hotel registry under his old name of "Doroteo Arango" and talked with him over coffee at a café nearby. He discovered that Villa, now rebounding from despair, was smuggling carrier pigeons into his room and dispatching them at night to his followers in Chihuahua.

Meanwhile, in Mexico, events continued to happen fast. Huerta became *"El Presidente"* in February, 1913, and three or four days later Madero was murdered. News of Madero's assassination stirred "Doroteo Arango" to anger, persuading him to re-enter the fray.

He then sent a message by carrier pigeons into the interior of Mexico to assure his men that he would meet them at the *"presa,"* a dam near Chihuahua City, to carry on the war against Huerta. And this he did, on March 5. To his amazement, he found that as many as three thousand soldiers had heeded his call. From these soldiers, he set about the creation of the fantastic *"Dorados"* as his own bodyguards, selecting about three hundred prized men. The *Dorados* were organized near Chihuahua City, although they came from everywhere. Proved friends like Rodolfo Fierro, the "Butcherer," Martin López, and Tómas Urbina were included, as well as new men like Lorenzo Avalós, from the state of Coahuila, and Nícolas Fernandez, of the city of Torreón. Once more he had an army; once more fortune smiled on him.

La oportunidad? This, surely, was the right time.

Now he made no mistakes about his good luck. He rode the crest of his popularity warily. When his aid was sought by a great leader, he remembered the four months of jail in Mexico City and the long period of hiding at El Paso. When General Carranza rushed to him for aid against Huerta, he that day waxed a lot more wily. For the time being, he told Carranza, he preferred to operate in northern Mexico alone and to take orders from no one. He acted friendly but independent. Silently to himself, he swore to run the war his own way.

Rid of Carranza, he slipped back naturally into his guerrilla tactics. He took hours now to mull over his plans. His first thought was to assault Chihuahua City, but when his ancient enemy Orozco went there, he struck at once upon a better, a more daring idea. He would, he reasoned, "jump" past Chihuahua City and pounce upon the strategic border city of Juárez, where he was well known and well liked. Besides, there he could buy ammunition from El Paso. And after that? *Ay,* after that he could turn around and descend heavily upon Chihuahua City to annihilate Orozco and then, newly fired with that victory, blaze a ruddy trail through Jiménez, Torreón, and Celaya to the capital of Mexico itself. *El León del Norte* felt drunk with excitement.

Shortly before Villa's attack, Juárez was commanded by Generals Francisco Castro and Fernando Trusy Aubert. Villa's old friend, Otto Schuster, entertained General Aubert and his entire staff one night (November 10, 1913) with a drama and a beer party at the Crawford Theatre, in El Paso. General Aubert responded by inviting the Americans to a banquet in their honor four nights later at the Black Cat Cafe, on Sixteenth of September Avenue in Juárez. Several members in the Gilmore Brown Stock Company, Brown himself, his leading lady, Virginia Lykens, and the actors Mr. and Mrs. Armstrong, accompanied Mr. Schuster and his chauffeur, Charles Seggerson, to Juárez. They arrived just before midnight; and all entered the café except Mr. Seggerson, who explained, "I didn't sleep much last night; you go on and have a good time, and I will wait for you in front of the café and sleep a little while in the car." The guests went in to dine with the General and his aides, on turkey *molé* and the trimmings. At two in the morning they had finished their Mexican cigars and were singing the *Miserere* from *Il Trovatore* when an armed band of twenty men, led by five officers, burst into the dining hall. In the confusion General Aubert and nine of his staff escaped, but the American group and three Mexican officers, Captains Cortinas, Contreras, and Torres, were captured. Later, when quiet ensued, General Villa came in person to the Black Cat and freed the Americans, saying: "You Americans are going back to El Paso. I am sending you to the bridge with a bodyguard, so you will get there safely." As they walked out of the café, they saw a bloody spectacle. The figure of Charles Seggerson slumped over the steering wheel of the car. Three bullets had passed through his body, and they had not heard the shots while singing the *Miserere*. Neither had they known of Villa's successful entry into the city.

In exactly three hours, early on this morning of November 14, Villa had overrun Juárez, his first step toward dominating Mexico. He had sent a fake telegram to beguile the Federalists into thinking he remained in Chihuahua City while actually he surprised and overwhelmed them by unloading three thousand men from a freight train he had sent. In this second sacking of Juárez, Villa permitted pillaging and gory massacre. As soon as he could, he deported all the Spaniards in Juárez to El Paso, including Don Francisco Alonzo and his ten-year-old son, a youth later to star in Hollywood as Gilbert Roland. But that same day he executed some seventy-five Federalist officers. One of them, Captain Contreras, of General Aubert's staff, directed his own execution. He circled his heart with charcoal before facing the twenty-man firing squad and then recited in a firm voice: *"Atención! Armas al hombro! Apunten!—Fuego!"* He fell face forward, twitched twice from side to side, and then expired.

The Mexican *Federalistas* could do nothing about the massacre that was a sequel to the Black Cat Cafe incident, and the *gringos,* as usual, did very little. The next day, Mayor C. E. Kelly, of El Paso, who once had disarmed Pancho when he was temporarily incensed with Colonel Giuseppi Garibaldi, met General Villa at the Stanton Street Bridge to arrange for the welfare of Americans still stranded in Juárez. General Hugh L. Scott, chief of staff of the United States Army, and George Carrothers, personal agent of President Wilson, also conferred with him on the border, where everything soon reverted to its former peacefulness.

Juárez became entirely Villa's city, and on it he left the permanent stamp of his personality. He paved its streets, rebuilt its hospitals, kept up its railroads, and collected its import and export duties. To his credit, he raised the salaries of school teachers, kept the peace, and administered wisely. To his discredit, he levied tribute on Americans, taxed the people to the breaking point, and licensed gambling and prostitution. For good or ill, he ruled as lord and master of the city of Juárez for one year. He made the most of his opportunity, purchasing supplies and munitions from cities as far away as New York, to which he sent his brother, Hipolito, as a buyer, and from as close as El Paso, to which he constantly sent his representatives for all kinds of necessities. He rented a home for his wife on Oregon Street, in El Paso, for her safe-keeping. She and a Mrs. Del Campo sold soda water and candy down town to get money to aid her husband's wounded soldiers. He made friends with General "Black Jack" Pershing and went big game hunting with him in the Sierra Madre. His army expanded, trained itself to a fighting edge, strutted up and down the *avenidas* in bright new uniforms. Soon it was restless for action.

As a Christmas present for the *peones,* Villa gave Chihuahua City back to its people in December. He demolished the enemy with 4,000 men and met the welcome accorded a deliverer. True to his political banner, "Savior of the Poor," he now allowed each *peon* to have a plot of land as his own. Now, day by day, the ranks of his army swelled with enthusiastic recruits. Christmas, the New Year of 1914, and Saint Valentine's Day passed in merriment. The tragedy known as the Cumbre Tunnel disaster occurred near Pearson early in February, it is true, in which all fifty-one train passengers, including Americans, of the Mexican Northwest Railway burned to death in the explosion. The dynamiter proved to be Maximo Castillo, so that Villa, for once, felt no involvement. Suddenly the month of March, blowing up clouds of desert sand, beat upon his consciousness, and bestirred him from his luxury. The *Dorados* stomped about, eager and impatient, as the bugles rang out again. A hero of the people answered the call of destiny.

The next objective was the big one—Mexico City— but the city of Torreón loomed as a stumbling block in the way. Pancho and his "international" army, including such writers as John Reed and Lincoln Steffens, hit the outskirts of the city in March—and stalled. For days the carnage went on. The *Dorados* grew fanatical. High on *marihuana,* or something, they fought like demoniac spirits. They stormed the entrenchments. They ground out yards and still got nowhere. Then they staggered about here and there confused. The Carranzistas dashed through the streets; then the Villistas.

> *Ay,* there go the Carranzistas . . .
> Who comes here?

Why, the Villistas.
Ay, Pancho Villa; *ay,* Pancho Villa.

Villa's forces struck again and again, in the bloodiest slaughter of the Revolution, before Torreón capitulated. Seven thousand men—and women—died in that battle.

Well done, Pancho Villa!
His heart did not waver;
He took the strongest fort
On the hill at Torreón.

After that, it took a while for the victor to lick his wounds. But the enemy had been, at least for the nonce, either defeated or dispersed.

Next the rebel tide easily overwhelmed Huerta, and he abdicated, escaping to El Paso. His successor became *pro tem* President Eulalio Gutiérrez. In November, 1914, Villa and his *Dorados* went by train to Mexico City to confer with Gutiérrez. The world of Mexico was his for the taking. Everywhere the *Dorados* were wined and feted. Villa bared his dark head, kinky as a Negro's, to repeated ovations. *"Ay, Pancho Villa! Ay! Ay-yay!"* In a camelhair overcoat he visited the tomb of Madero and stood there weeping hot, blinding tears. When he reached this zenith of his fame, what went on in his mad head? Did he remember the Rancho Rio Grande? old Ignacio Parra? the fat doubloons of *oro* hidden in the Sierra Madre? the concupiscent Cuca? Ordinarily his face, with its buck teeth, looked adenoidal; now it was wreathed with the smile of a conqueror. Speaking with his rural accent, he publicly addressed his *Dorados*. "Always consider yourselves great," he told them; "never permit anyone to humiliate you. . . . Fight for justice and be men." He talked "big." Was he not *el gran hombre?*

The populace, tumultuously favoring Pancho Villa, straightway tendered him everything. The people offered him the presidency, and he, in humility, declined it. He told them, or tried to tell them, that he was a simple man and did not have the proper qualifications for so high an office. He hedged, saying perhaps yes and perhaps no. Actually there was a worrisome thing behind him, and Pancho for once really had "something" on his mind. The rumor now flying in the air said that the United States had turned against him to look with favor on Carranza. Something more than a rumor assured him that one mighty combination now opposed him, because Carranza and Obregón then joined their two forces. Just when he had caught *la oportunidad* by the tail, the structure of his fame threatened to collapse. He could not rule as a dictator of the Republic so long as the mighty forces of General Carranza and General Obregón arrayed themselves against him. So he declined the offer. . . . Perhaps, later, conditions might be different? Right now he had things to do. As the year 1915 came round the bend, he hastened to Juárez, swearing he would take care of Carranza:

> *Con las barbas de Carranza,*
> *Voy a hacer una toquilla*
> *Pa' ponersela al sombrero*
> *De su padre Pancho Villa.*

With the whiskers of Carranza,
I'm going to make a hat band,
To put it on the sombrero
Of his 'boss' Pancho Villa.

Back in Juárez, General Villa immediately organized an army to fight Obregón. He counted on his old
friend, Tomás Urbina, to bring reinforcements. His new
friend, Felipe Ángeles, advised him against fighting
without reserves but finally agreed to string along with
him. In the spring of 1915, he contacted the enemy, under Obregón, at the ill-fated battle of Celaya, which he
lost. He met defeat because Obregón held the "number
one" positions and because Carranza remained in the
north to cut off the rebels' supplies. Urbina's failure to
come to the rescue with reinforcements also contributed
to the debacle. In the opinion of admirers, who never
liked to picture him in defeat, he lost the battle without
the Federalists being able to win a victory. Villa re-
treated in fine order and evacuated his wounded. A *"Corrido Villista"* expressed the sadness of the vanquished
Dorados:

Goodbye "Villistas" over there in Celaya;
Their blood they gave with much valor.
Goodbye, my beautiful Chihuahua,
Parral, Juárez, Lerdo, and Torreón.

After the loss of Celaya, Pancho once more withdrew,
dejectedly, to Juárez. He had plenty to think about,
and in many ways this defeat was the least of his troubles. Too many disreputable stories were circulating
about him in too many places. People disliked the way

he recruited his men, saying that when a man refused to join him, he cut off the *hombre's* head and strung him to a tree. People claimed that he was not religious, saying over and over again that in Santa Rosalia de Camargo he thrice ordered gunmen to fire upon the church, executing them when they did not, and desisted only when he went up to the church and saw the vision of Santa Rosalia himself. People kept saying this, that, and the other. The worst of it was that the *gringos* were beginning to talk, too. The *gringos* angered slowly but they always remembered. Here it was the summer of 1915, and he still heard whisperings about that Englishman, William S. Benton, who had "died" last year—so long ago, indeed, as February, 1914. *Ay, ay*—now that the attitude of the United States grew perceptibly cooler each day—he recalled all too well the dispute between Benton, a cattleman of Chihuahua, and his own right-hand "Butcherer," Rodolfo Fierro. Why could not people—even *gringos*—understand that his behavior was for the benefit of his country; that Benton represented, in his eyes, a foreign exploiter?

Having grown weary of seeing his cattle stolen, Bill Benton had gone straight to the bandit's headquarters in Juárez. To prime his courage and steady his gun hand, the Englishman had become a little "high" from drinking *sotol*. At the General's headquarters, the bodyguards introduced Benton as a man from England. The guards withdrew behind curtains near their *jefe*'s desk. Villa remained seated. Benton threatened to do something drastic unless the bandit stopped stealing his cattle.

"Who is this England?" Pancho asked.

"England is the most powerful country in the world," Benton answered.

"I am the rooster of this cage," Pancho said. "England is far from here. This is another country. Who is the rooster in that pen?"

"The King of England," Benton answered, half drunk and red with anger as he stood near the bandit.

About that time the Englishman made a move to get his handkerchief. With a burst of gunfire, somebody (probably the "Butcherer" Fierro) shot Benton down in his tracks. Nobody ever knew precisely what occurred, because another version of the story said that Villa took Benton to the country, made him dig a six-by-three hole in the ground, and then shot him down so that he fell into his own self-made grave.

In late summer (1915) Pancho's spirits plumbed the nadir before rebounding with a fresh plan to salvage everything. Much of his trouble had passed away, he knew. He had somehow survived the "Benton affair" by the skin of his teeth. Perhaps the supremacy could be regained by sacking the state of Sonora and then advancing southward to Sinaloa. His friend of the moment, Governor José Mario Maytorena, had promised him strong aid in Sonora. Moreover, he now enjoyed the good graces of the *gringos,* particularly those of General Hugh L. Scott. This favor cost him something. In August, he met General Scott at the home of J. F. Williams, on west Rio Grande Street in El Paso, and there publicly rescinded his earlier order confiscating the American mining interests in Mexico. The idea of the Sonoran campaign appealed to him so insistently that, in September, he placed Juárez under the command of his ordnance chief, Colonel Tomás Ornelas.

He next began to concentrate his forces at Casas Grandes. There, on September 15, he reviewed an army of no less than fifteen thousand men, equipped with forty cannons and seventy-five machine guns.

La oportunidad!

With the boldness of a lion, Pancho, on September 16, sent two thousand soldiers through dangerous Pulpito Pass—a narrow path through the Sierra, twenty-five feet wide and five miles long. By the end of October, 1915, the entire army with its supplies had come through the Pass. A mere handful of enemy forces could easily have stopped the entry and voided passage. Surely destiny fought by Pancho's shoulder! Ahead lay the *adobe* village of Agua Prieta, guarded by a *pelado* general named Calle—or was it Calles?—a nobody whose forces General Francisco Villa's outnumbered five to one. According to his scouts, all Sonora was his for the taking. *Ay! Pancho. Ay! Ay-yay! Una oportunidad* much to his liking. . . . *Qui-qui-ri-qui,* a red rooster crowed lustily.

CHAPTER 9

Chimera

Upon arriving in Sonora in October, 1915, Villa found his new ally already at war with the enemy. Governor Maytorena held the forces of General Calles and Benjamin Hill in a half-moon defense at the border town of Naco. The forces of Maytorena entrenched themselves eight hundred yards away, and from this vantage point lay siege to the *pueblo*.

Only one broad street divided Naco, Sonora, and Naco, Arizona, so that in the fighting shells naturally fell across it on the American town. As the fighting progressed, however, the Mexicans seriously damaged properties on the Arizona side, because they fired into store buildings and residences as well as the transcontinental trains of the El Paso-Southwestern Railroad. Villa's firm friend, General Scott, local United States Commander, reported that gunfire from Mexico killed or wounded fifty-four Americans. The Arizonans passed from fright to anger, being mightily concerned with having either to seek shelter in the basements of their houses or to sleep on mattresses on the floor to protect themselves from bullets coming through the windows. President Woodrow Wilson quickly empowered General Scott to arrange a truce, which he did. It was Villa himself who persuaded the otherwise recalcitrant May-

torena to quit the siege. This indicated clearly Villa's
desire to continue his friendly relations with the United
States. When Maytorena returned to the capital at Hermosillo, Calles withdrew to Agua Prieta.

For about a month after that, the Villistas, a *peon*
army, did nothing. Villa's rabble included *soldaderas*
with their ragged children and puling infants. They
camped with the soldiers in the open or at times in little
canyons nestling in the hills. All of them lived a direc-
tionless, nomadic existence, wandering about here and
there from dry arroyos into green valleys, slaughtering
"stray" beeves and "picking up" provender wherever
they could. Occasionally they shot a deer or a bear. They
had to do so, for Villa's old fault as a military man continued with him: he always ran low on supplies. Another
problem could have been water, but this the Villistas
solved by hauling water for themselves and their animals from a nearby ranch in Arizona. As the slow, warm
days dragged by, Villa's nondescript "army" grew in-
creasingly less inclined to fight, much less to start anything. They swarmed like bees, a multitude of fifteen
thousand souls, women and ripe girls and children,
peones and Indians and *Dorados,* encamped upon the
earth of Sonora. The women nursed their crying babes
and cooked *frijoles;* the moon-bosomed girls made pro-
miscuous love; the *peones* swigged their *sotol* and waxed
fat from inaction. Villa's rabble included long-haired
Indians, some of whom smoked *marihuana* at night and
threw fits or danced wildly about the campfires. Everywhere the "campers" reeked of filth and, worse still, of
gluttony and sloth. Maybe there would be a *baile* at
night. If he got drunk enough, a Villista might carol a
verse from a *corrido:*

Yo soy soldado de Pancho Villa. . . .
I am a soldier of Pancho Villa.
I am the most faithful of the *"dorados."*
It matters not if I lose my life
Or that I die for him against any man.

What Villa did at night was not too much of a question, since he was forever up to something. Pancho—the indefatigable rooster! Sometimes he stayed away all night; sometimes for a night and a day. He lived heroically, becoming a superman, a *vaquero* who traveled hard and far. He had to keep a *remuda* in order to have a fresh mount when he needed one. Some mornings *Siete Leguas* would stand up shakily at camp where his master had dismounted, completely lathered with a sweaty suds. Perhaps that night he had spurred toward the Rio Grande and at a midway point between Chihuahua and Sonora held a rendezvous with his wife, María Luz Corral de Villa. Perhaps he had ridden far away to enact a murder of revenge. One of his followers left behind him in Chihuahua proved to be a traitor. In Juárez, during his absence, Colonel Ornelas surrendered the city to Carranza without a struggle, and so Villa had to shoot him. But on most evenings Pancho and a *compañero* or two probably galloped rapidly southward to Hermosillo, the Sonoran capital, as they sang once again *"Me voy":*

I go to see the girl of my love
To contemplate her lovely countenance.

All he needed to spur his comrades to join him was to have his guitarist, Ochoa, begin *"La Jesusita":*

Let's go to the dance and see how lovely it is,
Where it is illumined with twenty lanterns,
Where the girls show their pretty legs,
Where they dance with great abandon.

In those days the wandering minstrel, Pancho, exhibited
everything except a fighting temper.

So it went through the month of October.

On November 1 General Calles, tired of waiting, decided to locate Villa's army. Calles, well-protected in
Agua Prieta, had hoped that Villa would launch the
attack. This situation obtained: north of Agua Prieta
lay Douglas, Arizona; in all the other directions, unin-
habited plains; and at a distance, the mountains. No one
could approach nearer than ten miles without being seen
clearly from Agua Prieta. Calles organized his defenses
well. The small rectangular town was walled in on four
sides by trenches. Outside upreared strong barbed-wire
entanglements above "planted" mines. So compact were
the fortifications that three thousand men sufficed to
guard the town satisfactorily. In fact, the enemy would
be unable to use many more than that in his attack, for
the bullet-proof reason that there existed no room in
which to maneuver his troops. In addition, Calles had
at his beck and call abundant supplies and, more important yet, strong reinforcements, because the American
government had just permitted Carranzistas to come
from Juárez to Agua Prieta *via* the United States railroad from El Paso to Douglas. General Calles stood
rearing to go. He knew that the Villistas lurked out of
sight somewhere off in the hills fast by. Unable to re-
strain his impatience any longer, Calles struck the first
blow. To locate Villa, he fired his largest cannon, its

thunderous echoes rolling out amid fire and smoke and reverberating to the distant hills. Instantly the Villistas returned the fire.

Hastily Pancho's rabble manned their weapons and soon began to discharge their forty cannons and seventy-five new machine guns. They gave a creditable account of themselves in this prelude to the battle, returning blast for blast. The artillery duel lasted for two hours, at the end of which the *Federales* slackened their fire. As it was early in the day, Pancho determined to launch the first of three staccato attacks. A strong wind blew coldly out of the desert, as storm clouds marshalled themselves threateningly in the distance, yet he issued the order to attack. Soon, less than ten miles away, Calles saw an irregular line of thousands of horsemen stampeding in his direction amid an enveloping cloud of gray dust.

As the Villistas advanced nearer, dust blew in the cold wind over the dirty plains and began to shroud from view the huge, ill-organized cavalry. At that distance they looked like grayed spirits from the other world, not like the hard-bitten *Dorados* of Chihuahua. When they reached the town, the wind drove the swarming hordes of Villistas apart and left them suddenly firing confusedly as much at themselves as at their foes. Dust hooded their flaming red eyes; grit lacerated their open mouths; yet they peered here and there, yelling like demons. They shouted *"Viva Villa! Viva Mexico!"* Once they gained the main street of the town, a veritable inferno of noise, a clap-trap of nerve-shaking sound assaulted their ears: store signs swept to the ground, hurtled and banged from side to side down the narrow streets. For them it became *el calle de la muerte,* a narrow street of merciless death. Unable to hear Villa's orders because of the pandemonium, they moved about aimlessly. While this happened, the calm *Federales,* protected by their bulwarks, sent volley after volley of well-directed missiles into the disintegrating, collapsing ranks of the rebels. Agua Prieta turned into a slaughtering place of wind and smoke, of gray dust, and of short, stabbing flames of gunfire.

During the two brief lulls in the three staccato daylight attacks, the unpaved streets of the *adobe* hamlet of Agua Prieta seemed to lift themselves solidly up to become undistinguishable from the dust-laden air. Corridors between *adobe* huts choked with swirling dust. At the end, ragged Villistas, many of them long-haired Indians who looked like women, littered the earth in every conceivable posture of death or dying, a few feeble ones gesturing grotesquely in the final throes of their last agony. The *Federales* lost men, too, but much fewer. A brave Federal officer, First Lieutenant Antonio Moreno, for whom a monument was later built where he succumbed, led a band of Calles's men afoot against Villa's horsemen, all being trampled to death against the windswept ground. Little by little, a stench of blood and horse dung began to filter through the air, and granulated sand to mingle with the acrid odor of gunpowder. Early in the battle, many people fleeing to Douglas for safety were killed or wounded. Stray bullets dropped sporadically in Douglas, where most citizens quickly sought cover. Fantastic incidents occurred. A stray bullet hurtled through a window to cut off the tail of a canary. Everywhere windows cracked; telephone lines clattered down; automobiles collided against obstructions or each other. The Americans huddled in corners or on the floors, expecting any moment to see the Villistas riding madly into Douglas to tear down their doors and massacre them where they crouched in fear.

Twice more the formless body of innumerable Villistas charged the impenetrable fortress which Agua Prieta was that day. As soon as they charged, everybody yelled *"Allí viene Pancho!"* for there came Villa, sure enough. The coughing, sputtering, clay-faced horsemen who reached the middle of the town churned chaotically up and down the dirt-darkened streets, running their frantic, unseeing mounts head-on into each other as a deep indigo pall of mingled gunpowder and dust rose to the Sonoran sky. Blindly the Villistas fired at random in a tumult of abject fear and hapless confusion. They suffered a pandemonium come again. Once the silhouette of a mounted Villista horseman loomed in the darkening blue sky, on a slight rise of the terrain, before his yellow Palomino reared upward as the brown Villista, drilled in the back, pitched sidelong into a dark ditch of broken red wagons and rusty, torn metal.

Safe behind their ramparts, the *pelados,* the low caste Federal soldiers, easily picked off the plunging rebel riders, one by one, plugging the stumbling *hombres* who had somersaulted from their horses before they could run for a house or store to hide in. The last scene was a horrendous holocaust, with red corpses riddled by bullets and bruised by horses' hooves lying everywhere. The maddened mounts, careening this way and that as they trailed their saddles or their fallen dead masters, screamed and pitifully whinnied, pawing the silt-heavy air until finally they broke tempestously away into a headlong gallop for the distant mountains. The storm did not cease until long after the dark curtain of a bitterly cold night descended. Step after soft step an appalling quiet then settled over everything.

After nightfall, the Villistas attended to their wounds, patched their clothes, mended their saddles—and wet their whistles. *Sotol* irrigated their dust-filled throats, burning away the shock of the recent defeat. In the dark night, *marihuana* cigarettes spurted with tiny red tongues of fire and crackled a little as the flames ate into the hay-like weed. Numb fatigue would have driven them to slumber had they not continued to swig the fiery *sotol* and draw upon their *loco* weeds. By midnight, the drunken, drugged Villistas, now unconscious of their bruised limbs and wounded bodies, were wide awake and in a violent mood. They commenced to prepare a ferocious assault upon their foes before the crack of dawn.

Back in the hills—out of sight of the enemy—Pancho studied his map beside a small fire and laid out plans for a final raid, one designed to demolish his foes. Now and then a Yaqui Indian, of the large band he had pressed into his service, stepped away from the intent circle of men who scrutinized the map and threw the dried trunk of an *agave* plant on the fire before it began to smolder. The chunk of *agave* then burned briskly, casting a clear light in the direction of the mapgazers who perched on their haunches about the outspread square of paper, at which the men, from time to time, pointed with gesticulations and excited eyes. Perhaps his oldest friend, Miguel Trillo, helped him at the last to come to a decision. For, finally, Pancho struck the map with his fist, picked it up, and spoke rapidly to his men. The Indians padded about so softly that he decided to send them forth ahead to infiltrate the enemy trenches before a frontal assault in force could be suspected.

The bareheaded Yaquis, their tangled hair trailing down their cheeks and necks, crept toward the barbed wire entanglements with knives between their teeth, to start the surprise attack. The intrepid Indians acted like wild men completely out of their heads from inhaling the *marihuana*. But at the minute they reached the barbed wire fortifications, somebody from the plaza in Douglas threw three giant spotlights upon the prostrate Indians wriggling forward on their bellies. Two American Negro soldiers, who had managed to get machine guns against the orders of their commander, at this juncture began to spatter the Villistas from the top of a house with a rat-a-tat-tat of machine gun fire. Immediately the Indians rose to a crouch and headed for the barbed wire. The *marihuana* gave them superhuman strength. So frenzied were they with the drug that some of them succeeded in breaking the wire with their hands. The fight proceeded unequally, for each time an Indian cleared the fortification the two Negro soldiers picked him off cleanly in the glare of the giant spotlights. For an unreal half-hour the Yaquis jumped and plunged under the spotlight, some of them clearing the fortfications only to perish under the merciless spurt of the machine guns while others, turning to run toward the mountains, became entangled in the barbed wire and died from gun shots. Had it not been for the American soldiers, who killed many of the Villistas, Pancho's daring plan might well have succeeded. Under the unequal conditions, the suicidal onslaught finally subsided. The Carranzistas finished the attack by machine gun action with a series of fusillades, concluding with a superfluous round of well-placed artillery fire.

The next day nothing more came from the Villistas. On November 3, Villa seemed to be massing for a formidable assault, but, on the morning of the fourth, observers spotted him retreating toward Naco.

After the battle, people began to piece together details about the famous leader of the siege. Villa's wounded suffered so terribly from their beating at Agua Prieta that George Kingdon, company manager of a big copper camp at Cananea, sent over two physicians, Doctors Thigpen and Miller, to the bandit's aid. Villa received them warmly, and they were well started on their work when he learned that President Wilson had allowed Federal troops to pass through American territory from Laredo and El Paso to Douglas. Instantly Villa became angry at this "partiality" shown by the United States government. General Scott later defended Pancho's reactions. "We permitted Carranza to send his troops through the United States by our rails to crush Villa. I did what I could to prevent this but was not powerful enough. I had never been put in such a position in my life. After Villa had given up millions of dollars at the request of the state department, expressed through me, they made him an outlaw. He was a wild man who could not be expected to know the difference between the duties of the state and war departments, and might very well have thought that I double-crossed him had he not had the confidence in me that he did."

Villa did distrust the *gringos* from Arizona. He called the American physicians, Doctors Thigpen and

Miller, to him and asked if they masqueraded as spies. They denied the charge, swearing that they had come for purely humanitarian reasons. Villa cast them in prison, anyhow, and threatened them with execution. Each morning for several days the rebels brought them out to be shot—and each day Villa changed his mind, whereupon they were returned to their cells to await execution the next day. The copper company learned of this and sent representatives to secure their release. After some negotiations—and the payment of $25,000 for so-called "taxes"—the doctors secured their release near Saus, several miles from Naco. Before reaching the safety of Arizona, they almost succumbed from exhaustion. Dr. Miller, a very heavy man, later died as a result of the experience.

While the Villistas holed up around Naco, they constantly demanded supplies from the miners to the south in Cananea. They "poached" upon the cattle of their enemies. Once three teams set out for the borderline from Cananea for flour. The Villistas captured the teams, teamsters, and the flour, but the teamsters subsequently made their escape. Following this, the copper company deemed it wise to furnish the outlaws with supplies and delivered a carload of flour to the hungry troops, who were practically out of provisions. After that Villa demanded fifteen hundred head of steers for food and 175 horses for his *Dorados*. In exchange for these the cattle manager secured a promise that Villa would not destroy the property of the ranch as well as a *"salvo-conducto"* to travel about the ranch in safety. The Villistas wandered about for a while. They started once to overrun a farm at San Pedro, but when the cattle manager showed his *"salvo-conducto,"* they agreed not to demolish the farm but only to use the hay stored there. On the arrival of the Carranzistas a little later, the robbers fled to the safety of their sanctuary, the hills of Sonora.

While Generals Obregón and Calles trailed them, the Villistas raided unprotected Cananea and demanded money. The head of the bank, at the point of a gun, which made him extremely nervous, opened the vault and gave Villa all the cash on hand—about one hundred thousand *pesos*. Did he buy ammunition with this from a storekeeper in Columbus, New Mexico? Did he hide it in the hills? Nobody ever knew for certain what he did with his loot.

The Villistas bivouacked in Cananea about three days. Rankling from the "treachery" of the United States in aiding their enemies, they regarded anything American as fair loot and stole horses right and left. Villa stood up in the public square in Cananea, on an elevated platform, and made two speeches trying to rouse the people of Sonora to his cause. Then he spoke at Terrenate. But his speeches, delivered with his rural Chihuahua accent, left the Sonorans cold, availing him nothing. Unlike the citizens of Parral and Juárez, in the state of Chihuahua, the residents of this western state, who liked the "smooth," educated Carranza, paid him no heed, viewing him as a filthy bandit and utter ignoramus. The only thing left for him to do, since his rabble now lived on the land as they had in their early bandit days, was to divide his multitude into three groups, for they found it easier to forage for supplies when they moved in smaller, more maneuverable, bodies.

He gave the three groups instructions to migrate southward in order to converge on Hermosillo. But it worked out otherwise; and his careful plans went askew.

One group departed through Ojo de Agua, a watering place, and, realizing that the odds were stacked against them, simply continued on back homeward to Juárez. A second group headed southward *via* Nogales Ranch; and, its members gradually dispersing themselves, failed to meet Villa at Hermosillo as promised. The third group, commanded by Villa, caused a lot of trouble before it pulled out of Sonora. Federal *rurales,* dressed in their regular tan uniforms, followed as hot on Villa's trail as they possibly could.

Pancho, to speed his getaway, grabbed two narrow-gauge trains from a copper company to take him to Puertocitos Pass, whence he intended to go on foot to Martinez and seize engines and cars to transport them onward to Nogales. They forced an American named E. B. Bean, a Mexican called "Pancho," and two firemen to run the train to Puertocitos. The Federalists following Villa traveled by wagon and confronted the Villistas at the Pass. Straightway the shooting began. On the pretense of looking for food, the Mexican called "Pancho" and the two firemen hid in one of the numerous tunnels at Puertocitos. But Bean had to go on with the rebels. One of Villa's officers, Colonel Beltram, personally shot the man without known reason, after which the Villistas escaped their pursuers and hurried on to the town of Martinez. They arrived in Martinez without further mishap, there entraining for Nogales.

Nogales, Sonora, and Nogales, Arizona, are twin cities of the border, divided only by a street, International Avenue. When Villa uttered threats that he would shoot up Nogales, Arizona, officials closed the international boundary to all traffic. American National Guardsmen, under Colonel Sage, set up barricades. This provoked the Villistas to threaten to blow up the *gringo* barricades. Pancho Villa, however, did not intend to launch a battle; instead, in his old guerrilla fashion, he merely pulled off another one of his raiding parties. They looted the stores of all their plunder, after which, when the *gringos* started to decimate their ranks with rifle shot, they loped easily out of town southward toward Hermosillo. For the next day or two the Villistas ate heartily, throwing what they did not want themselves to the rustic, grateful poor. They knew full well they could get more whenever they needed it.

Now, at Hermosillo, Villa expected to be joined by his friendly ally, Governor Maytorena. He had dispatched funds to him with which to buy much-needed ammunition. But Villa again proved unfortunate in his choice of friends. Like Tomás Urbina, Colonel Ornelas, and some of the rest, Maytorena cowardly betrayed General.Villa. Governor Maytorena showed himself to be much smarter than either Urbina or Ornelas, because when Villa arrived at Hermosillo, he had already escaped to Los Angeles with the money. Thus he found, unexpectedly, that Hermosillo, instead of being his for the asking, loomed as a fortress yet to be subdued. Half-heartedly, the dejected Villistas surrounded the capital of Sonora, and intermittently launched probing attacks from each side of their circle. General Villa must not have had his heart in the battle, because had he done so, he could have won hand over fist. The residents, ill equipped, moved about awkwardly, having so few soldiers that they transferred them by automobiles from one side of the town to the other whenever the lackadaisical Villistas attacked. Villa captured a sizeable number of prisoners in the environs of Hermosillo but never entered the capital. At last he quit the site and trekked westward for La Colorada. Here he encountered no armed opposition and conducted himself in his usual fashion: one moment he acted like a civilized man and in the next like a barbarian.

One atrocity which he committed there may best be told by a doctor who witnessed it: "I had been called to see the wife of Pedro Pinelli, an Italian mine operator in La Colorada. It was quite early in the morning, and when I arrived at the house Pinelli was sitting on the porch with Villa, to whom I was introduced and asked to sit down. During the conversation Villa asked me how long I had lived there and whether I had any enemies. I replied that I had none. He said it was strange having lived so long in one town that I had no enemies. Presently there appeared a group of men accompanied by soldiers on the opposite side of the arroyo where there was a large corral with a high adobe wall around it. Villa arose and ordered Pinelli and myself to accompany him, which, needless to say, we did, as by that time I realized that something unusual was to happen, and I had heard of Villa's reputation as a killer.

"We walked over to the group of men and soldiers. Villa spoke a few words, which I did not hear, to the soldiers, and the men were immediately lined up against the wall. Villa then personally shot and killed these eight men with his shooting iron, turned to us and said, 'This is what happens to enemies of Pancho Villa. People are your friends or your enemies. There can be no *neutrals.*'"

No doubt Villa rankled with disappointment after his enthusiastic campaign became a chimera. Probably he was both bloodthirsty and vengeful, yet the tales told of him sound incredible. The tallest one reported that, while leaving Sonora, he stopped at tiny San Pedro de La Cueva to massacre seventy-two old men and young boys. He lined up the hapless group and, since he was then short on ammunition, shot them endwise. He placed his rifle against the chest of the first and thus perforated as many as possible. When these fell, he fired again.

Villa's campaign drew to its sanguinary close in the region of Rubio and the memorable town of Santa Isabel. He dispersed his men at Santa Isabel in December, 1915, for the purpose of harassing the *Americanos* and Carranzistas. At this juncture the desperate Villa, beloved only by the peasants, hit the nadir of despair. There were no two ways about it—he was down and out.

CHAPTER 10

Columbus

In the first week of January, 1916, a group of Texas business men started south by rail from Juárez to operate the Cusihuiriachic mines below Chihuahua City. After the train left Chihuahua, a band of Villistas stopped it at Santa Isabel, ordering the Americans out. The bandits lined them up and shot them down. All slumped over, but one man lived to tell the tale. The thirteenth at the end of the line, he rolled down the side of the embankment and, crawling away into a patch of brown mesquite bushes, escaped. The train chugged on, leaving the corpses at the mercy of their slayers, who stripped and mutilated them. After the escapee arrived in Chihuahua, a special train sped to Santa Isabel to reclaim the bodies. When the people of El Paso heard of the atrocity, they went wild with anger. The city passed promptly under martial law, so that nobody could cross into Mexico at Juárez to wreak vengeance on innocent parties.

Since Villa had dispersed his followers around Rubio and Santa Isabel, the blame fell on his shoulders. Promptly he denied the charge. His subordinate, he explained, had grossly exceeded his order to plunder the train. It was the bad *hombre* named Martin López who commanded the murdering group, which included General José Rodríguez. When the Americans demanded that the gory sadists be punished, the Mexican government executed Rodríguez, in Chihuahua, on January 15, 1916, displaying the corpse in its bier at Juárez shortly afterwards for citizens of the United States to view publicly. The execution of the commander, López, did not occur until nearly six months later, well after the perpetration of the Columbus atrocity.

Guilty or innocent at Santa Isabel, Pancho now had to shy from public places and once more began to wander as an outlaw. His enemies, the Carranzistas, hot on his heels, denied him his home in Chihuahua so that he, making a costly blunder, struck out again to the west. Possibly he had a reason other than flight. Perhaps he went back to unearth gold or supplies hidden in the yellow hills or to haul away ammunition which he had already bought from a New Mexican storekeeper in Columbus.

Whatever the reason, he arrived in Palomas, a pueblo opposite Columbus, on March 1, having stopped off at the Hearst ranch, in Correlitos, a little earlier to harass and murder a member of the Polanco family there in charge. The Thirteenth Cavalry of the United States Army learned of his nearing Palomas long before his arrival, estimating his forces no closer than from three to five hundred men. A persistent but absurd rumor declared that he intended to cross the border there to entrain for Washington, D. C., to interview President Wilson.

Instead of going to the American capital, Pancho Villa brazenly raided Columbus in force on the morning of March 9, 1916, at 2:30 A. M., unaccountably taking the Thirteenth Cavalry by complete surprise. As a result, the residents spent three hours of agony and terror listening to bullets striking the houses and the fiendish shouts of *"Viva Villa! Viva Mexico! Muerte a los Americanos!* One of them, the physician, Doctor Roy E. Stivison, said: "In the lurid light of the burning Ritchie Hotel and the Lemmon store we could easily distinguish men running hither and thither, riderless horses veering about in all directions. The continuous firing, the shouting, the confusion continued until about seven o'clock." Doctor and Mrs. Stivison then "set out for the main part of town. We found our old friend and neighbor, James Dean, a grocery merchant, lying in the middle of the street, his body riddled with bullets. We found the body of Mr. Ritchie (the hotel manager). His wife later told us he had offered the Villistas all the money in his pocket ($50.00) if they would spare his life. They took the money, but also shot him down beside his hotel."

A visitor, Mr. J. R. Galusa, arriving in Columbus on the train during the final phase of the battle, saw that "The smoke-filled streets were littered with the dead and wounded, and many of the residents were fleeing on foot."

Another eye-witness, this time a sixteen-year-old boy named Arthur Ravel, was in the thick of the action and saw everything that happened to many of the residents. "We were in the Commercial Hotel building, and I seen Mrs. Ritchie, I think it was, in Mr. Walker's saloon, begging the Mexicans over there not to kill Mr. Ritchie. I heard one of the Mexicans; he said: 'Anything that looks like a white, kill him.' There was another Mexican down there—he was a very white complected fellow, too—and they thought he was an

American, and they took him down. The next day I heard they had killed him, too.

"While I was there I saw them when they took Mr. Walker. When they took Mr. Ritchie down, they took me down, too. We left the stairs last. I saw Mr. Ritchie when he walked out to the corner of the Commercial Hotel, where they killed him. Then they came to me. 'Wait, don't kill him yet,' they said. I walked down the street. I saw Mr. Ritchie kinda move. He said 'Humph,' just like that, as I passed him.

"There was a great big body of Mexicans there. Then they said, 'Here he is; what shall we do with him?' They said: 'You take him down to the store and let him open the bank, and then do with him whatever you please.'

"I was in the middle of two men. We walked up the main street where our store is. Bullets were flying in every direction; fires were going every place; you would see once in a while a man drop dead. I seen them loot our store and Mr. Walker's store, a hardware store, of saddles and so on, and hardware.

"We walked to the place where Mrs. Moore's store is, and somebody shot the Mexican who had me. The other Mexican that had me, he said: 'Don't get scared. We will get to the bank yet.' I said: 'All right.' I walked up that way to the corner of the drugstore and somebody shot him, and I was left all alone."

Still another resident, Mr. Lee Riggs, deputy collector of customs, was awakened on the morning of the raid by a shot. He put his wife and two children in blankets on the floor and used mattresses to protect them from the gunfire. When their five-months-old baby began to cry, he feared the invaders might detect the noise, for they were close by, yelling and shouting. He told Mrs. Riggs to stuff a towel in the baby's mouth to keep her from crying. The mother held the towel there as long as she dared, until the baby became limp. By that time, fortunately, the firing had ceased, so that Lee Riggs could take his wife and children to the hospital.

During the invasion what did the *gringo* soldiers do? Some of them reacted slowly because they had been drinking and had left their rifles chained and locked in a gun rack. Others reacted quickly. Lieutenant W. A. McCain killed one Mexican by hammering in his head with the butt of his pistol. Another soldier killed a Villista Indian with a baseball bat. A gun crew caught a batch of Villistas against a kitchen wall, giving them a burst of deadly fire at close range to get the advantage of lethal ricochets. But unarmed Americans, especially the women, fared badly, though Mrs. Moore, Mrs. Ryan, and others escaped with minor wounds. Bunk, a Negro water foreman of Oihital's ranch, fell captive. The American soldiers displayed bravery in saving as many citizens as they did. They quelled the riot before the crack of that red, fateful dawn of March 9.

All this time the master mind of the raid, once so glorious a figure in battle, hid behind an embankment in a ditch. His companion was a twelve-years-old *muchacho,* Jesus Paiz. Their contribution to this bloody foray was simply to hold the horses of the fighters. When at last the Americans organized themselves and ran the Mexicans out, Pancho Villa escaped unharmed. His companion stayed long enough to be wounded in the leg, captured, and taken to Albuquerque to a surgeon, Doctor M. K. Wylder.

Villa with his decimated "army" made off across the

border due south from Palomas to what he hoped was safety. But he found there no moment of restful concealment or opportunity to regroup his men. Colonel Frank Tompkins somehow managed, amid the confusion, to mount a cavalry body of thirty-two American riders. In the dim light of the early morning of March 9, he gave pursuit into Mexico, opening fire on the fleeing Mexicans. His troops instantly sighted some of the enemy in the rearguard, inflicting on them a loss of over thirty men and horses. Others of the Villistas sped away while this action took place, but Colonel Tompkins kept up the chase farther into the interior for eight hours, which enabled him to destroy a number of stragglers as well as more of the rearguard of Villa's fleeing raiders. Lacking supplies, the hastily-formed cavalrymen of Tompkins were obliged to return to their base in Columbus, but they showed the invaders they meant business as they observed on their trek homeward from seventy-five to one hundred Villistas killed and actually counted.

When the American cavalry troops re-entered Columbus, the disordered populace remained in a state of hysteria. *Gringo* soldiers picked up the bodies of Villistas they had shot in the streets and on the outskirts of town, piling hundreds of them on grotesque funeral pyres to cremate them. For a day or more the fires smoldered before dying down while even longer the acrid odor of burned flesh permeated the air. Military officials somehow succeeded in holding from the irate citizens thirteen Villista prisoners in their custody, these being shortly conveyed for their protection to Deming, New Mexico. A trial of sorts occurred there nearly three months later, and two of the guilty marauders met death by hanging. On June 9, Governor Larrazolo of New

Mexico, to the surprise of many people, pardoned the remaining eleven captives because they testified that they had not known they were fighting in the United States. Their testimonials may contain a germ of truth since they were ignorant *hombres* used to raiding along the border in blind obedience to orders. For days beforehand they had been foraging unopposed in the neighborhood of Palomas, which is from Columbus but a step across, not the Rio Grande, but a strip of borderground. From the raid, in any case, the Mexicans gained nothing valuable beyond a few dollars and perhaps some merchandise from the store of the Ravel Brothers, who may have provoked Villa's rancor in their failure to deliver supplies or ammunition which he had already paid for. Or they may have been high on *tequila* and started the raid in a moment of careless enthusiasm. In this connection, Colonel Rodríguez afterwards stated that his leader, Villa, issued the order of attack as a mere gesture of bravado. Whatever the cause, Columbus lay virtually demolished, so completely burned and pillaged that it never recovered its former vitality.

Villa headed due south in his flight, but when news of his assault on Columbus first reached El Paso, Texans thought that he might head on a straight line eastward. As Columbus is west and a trifle north of Juárez, military authorities feared he would traverse the winding Rio Grande at Smeltertown to cut across the campus of the old College of Mines, and then, to avoid doubling back or to gesture grandly, travel directly southward into El Paso down Mesa Street to Juárez. The militia at Fort Bliss prepared for a rescue, but of course Pancho never turned up.

Weeks after the atrocity, people foregathered to

theorize about Villa's motives. Some people believed
that the motive was revenge. Mr. A. Barcena G., who
was at Columbus, felt that Villa did this because earlier
in 1916 somebody poured kerosene on Villista prisoners
in the El Paso jail and burned them alive. He avowed
that on entering into New Mexico Villa shouted,
"Avenge our brothers—kill all the *gringos!*" The
United States customs officer in Columbus, Mr. Jack
Breen, said that Villa did not personally take part in the
action. Mr. Breen also rather doubted the story that
Villa's papers outlining the program of attack were
afterwards found on the site of battle. Revenge figured
as the theme in another theory. Shortly after Doctor
Henry T. Juen came to El Paso, in 1915, he heard that
Villa hated the *gringos* for turning their favor from him
to Carranza and swore to kill all of them he could. Doctor Juen said: "He meant it—and we knew it. That was
partly behind the Columbus raid."

In later depredations in Texas along the border, at
such places as Brownsville, Boquillas, and Glen Springs,
Villa had no guiding hand. His full responsibility for
the attack in New Mexico can not be doubted. At the
moment that Pancho fled to the hills to obliterate himself
from the international scene, little Columbus became the
focus of all eyes.

> And they say that on a paper
> With much malice was written:
> If you claim to have Villa's head,
> Rewards are offered in Columbus.

CHAPTER 11

Crossing the Border

Pancho Villa, *hombre* from the hills, had nine days in which to effect his getaway before "Black Jack" Pershing's Expeditionary Force crossed into Mexico on March 15, 1916, at noon. This was more of a headstart than this raider ordinarily had, and he made the best advantage of it. Thoroughly frightened, he hired the Ohioan, Mr. Royce G. Martin, to remove his wife, Luz, and their children to Cuba for sanctuary. After that, he waited in concealment amid the silences of the desert.

Several factors caused Pershing's delay. Not all Americans supported him despite the fact that England and France stood firmly with him. The Russian minister of affairs said: "I consider the Mexican question as concerning only the United States. In my opinion the only satisfactory solution is annexation, and the action Russia would see with approval." But the automobile tycoon Henry Ford did not regard the Columbus "affair" seriously, refusing to permit workers in his factories to answer the call to arms. Colonel McCormick, of Chicago, accused Ford of being "as anti-American as any pro-German." The statement involved him in a lawsuit in Michigan with Ford that dragged on until 1920, when the Colonel paid him a "token" settlement, not of the thousands demanded, but of one lone silver dollar.

People in the Southwest more speedily recognized the urgency of prompt retaliation, for they knew that conditions threatened to grow even worse. Villa himself had warned his *amigo* General Scott, in 1915, that Germany and Japan had proposed to him an alliance against the United States. From time to time, handbills from foreign presses appeared in El Paso in support of Villa's assertion, whereas somebody in Monterrey now disclosed a "plan of San Diego" to embroil the neighboring nations in war by a German plot." Pershing faced a delicate situation. Large scale conflict must be avoided at all costs; what he needed was the consent of the Mexican government to send a punitive expedition against an "international outlaw." For this reason he besought the aid of Carranza, who claimed that he also wanted to catch the bandit. Bespectacled Carranza consented with tongue in cheek, proving to be a hindrance rather than a help.

> *Ay!* Carranza tells them anxiously,
> If you are brave and want to pursue him,
> I extend you ample permission,
> So that you may learn how to die.

Under the circumstances "Black Jack" did a rather amazingly efficient job in mounting a strong pursuit only nine days after the onslaught on Columbus. He knew what he was doing and knew the man he chased. He hired as his main guide the scout, Alexander Robert Carson, who, in 1915, had been kidnapped by Villa and who, in 1916, had helped to bury the bodies of the Texans massacred at Santa Isabel. To cover the uncharted terrain thoroughly, "Black Jack" divided his

Expeditionary Force into East and West columns and proceeded methodically into the Mexican interior.

The soldiers of Pershing, largely raw recruits, encountered every imaginable mishap during their eleven months in Mexico. Carranza had promised assistance, but when they were once on the eve of apprehending Villa, the Carranzistas attacked them. Another time their Indian scouts reported him wounded—and Villa was, in the knee—but then the Indians misinformed them about his lair. At other times the Indians brought in blood-filled boots and bullet-riddled shirts as "proofs" that he had been killed. The two American columns of the Expedition got nowhere. The East column fanned out through cactus and desert, *pueblos* and smaller settlements, Ascención and Corralitos. The West meandered about among hills and plains to Culberson's Ranch and Ojitos. After some months, both columns converged at Casas Grandes only to split asunder a little later, with one heading south for Pearson, Cumbre, and Madera, and the other trekking southeastwardly for Guerrero, Aguascalientes, Ojos Azules, and Carrizal. Everywhere they went, men, women, and children built for them a storehouse of misinformation on the subject of the whereabouts of Pancho Villa.

In Mexico, the Americans got anything they wanted for a piece of candy, a *peso,* or a cigarette. If a *gringo* queried the *señores,* they replied eagerly, *"Sí,* we know Pancho. He stopped here last night. An hour ago he went to the south. *Sí,* the man we saw is the *hombre* you are after. He is a big fat man with a black mustache, and Carranza says he is a bastard. *Sí, sí,* we know Pancho." The Mexicans had a good time and liked the *gringos.* They hungrily ate their candy, gladly pocketed their money, and smoked the American cigarettes with a flourish of gusto.

The Pershing Expedition brought a "boon" to Mexico. The wants of the *gringos* were catered to and satisfied everywhere they went. Deep in the interior both humble *peones* and proud rural storekeepers welcomed the *Americanos*. Prices skyrocketed. *Cantinas* flashed new signs of *"Abierto"* or "Open All Night." Some *gringos* for the first time chewed on soft brown cactus candy, dropping its "oozy" syrup on their uniforms; munched on pink *tamales* that tasted sweet, not hot as on the border; inhaled the black smoke of ebony Mexican cigars as well as cigarettes like Alfonsos, Belmontes, and Virginias; submerged themselves in beer, *cervezas* like light Bohemia and Carta Blanca or dark Dos Equis and Modelo; and on the desert got as drunk as "sailors" on Latin firewater, on *mescal, sotol,* or *tequila*. In many restaurants they devoured "deer" meat that once ran in the streets barking; in better ones, roasted flesh of the blue Mexican quail or fat squabs of the multi-colored wild pigeons of Chihuahua. Eating highly spiced foods and "ripe" meats, some of them developed stomach ulcers. Occasionally an unacclimated Yankee from Minnesota or somewhere reported for "sick call" and regurgitated gobbets of half-done goat chops, swearing, falsely in every instance, that he had been maliciously poisoned. But the olive-skinned *señoritas,* in their parlors, smoldered at the touch of their rifle-hardened hands while the "loud" perfumes wiped away their memories of the stench of refuse and fresh human dung that gathered in the back streets outside the *serallos*.

Life was hard only when the Yankees, furnished with *pinole* as rations, marched or rode along the dirt roads, eating their "cornbread" and singing a verse they had composed about Pancho and his compatriot, López, who had led the Columbus raid:

> We left the border for Parral
> In search of Villa and López, his old pal.
> Our horses, they were hungry,
> And we ate parched corn.
> It was damn hard living
> In the state of Chihuahua
> Where Pancho Villa was born.

Villa, who hailed from Durango instead of Chihuahua, turned into a myth. On the records of his saga he added a figurative interlude, wherein he became celebrated as "The Wraith of the Desert." He epitomized the elusive, and fables sprang up from the data of his chase. One time Pershing's men would hear that he had died from his gunshot wound and already been buried in Santa Ana; the next they were told that he had survived it by cleansing his wound with a turkey feather which he drew through it. One day they would hear that he was too crippled to move because a Carranzista had spotted him at a distance dragging a horse away by a tight rope, had shot the rope into two pieces, and had seen the thief tumble backward from sight into a ditch; the next they learned that he had recovered and been almost captured beneath a water tank when he had run away with his rifle and turned to shoot a hole in the tank, whose gushing waters had then all but drowned his enemies below.

Maybe Carranza had not lied in his purported retort to a query from the *gringos* as to Villa's whereabouts: "I have the honor to inform you that, according to the information I have acquired and believe to be the truth, Villa is now found everywhere and nowhere." Gathered in the noonday sun, the *peones* went the Carranzistas one better, telling how, when he was about to be caught, he changed himself into an *agave* plant as Pershing's cavalry charged blindly by or how, tired of being pursued, he transformed himself into a little brown dog, reversed his course, and started in behind his attackers yelping and nipping at their heels. Their tallest yarn claimed that, in other emergencies, he put the horseshoes on his mounts backwards so that his enemies never knew whether he was going or coming.

He distinguished himself, during the epic chase by Pershing, as the most adept artist in the world at dodging his pursuers. He knew the hideouts in the Sierra Madre better than the average man knows the contents of his trousers' pockets and holed up in convenient watering places, guffawing at the amateurish scouting of the green Yankee recruits. To mislead them, he tied tree branches behind his wagons, that wiped away the wheel tracks as his Villistas rattled and rolled into a blue oasis like Ojos Azules and disported themselves gayly with brown-eyed girls. In this place or that he "borrowed" *becerros* from the *rancheros* and buried all the carcasses of the beeves but one or two to beguile Pershing into thinking only a handful of wandering outlaws had fed themselves near the ranch. After someone wounded him in the leg beneath his left knee, he once barely avoided capture, but in spite of his handicap he still eluded his enemies. *Peones* tell how the *gringos* came storming over the desert, fast on his trail. Suddenly the trail grew cold; they could find no more hoofprints of his horse. The track vanished, not from magic, but because he had killed and buried his mount before going to his hiding place on foot. Afterwards, from a cave in the hills close by, he safely watched his pursuers mill around ineffectually. On other occasions, when he fled precipitately into the stygian black nights of Chihuahua, with Pershing's best-drilled equestrians drawing nigher and nigher, small guiding lights spurted in the windows from burning candles of *peon* families he once had fed or befriended. Pancho, the grand guerrilla fighter, operated with consummate ease in the copper-colored Sierra Madre.

The humble people of Mexico also tell how, at other stages of the chase, the Villistas mingled in the larger cities with the populace, from which they were undistinguishable minus their cartridge belts characteristically strapped across their chests. Later Villa himself contended that his men, unsuspected by anybody, had mixed with the Americans at will and even attended Western "shoot-'em-up" movies with Pershing's officers. All through the winter he eluded his seekers, to move about here and there mysteriously in hideaways in the hills, so that the trail of Pershing in Mexico as he pursued Villa was as full of windings as the tracks of a sidewinder snake. Villa was able to rest, to regain strength, as the Expeditionary Force careened willy nilly in no certain direction.

Soon a rested Pancho bestirred himself for quick, brutal action.

On January 7, 1917, Villa raided Camargo, sometimes known as Santa Rosalia. In this raid he murdered Chinese, Federal *soldaderas,* and civilian women— about three hundred people in all. Mr. Caterino Navarro, of El Paso, explained the action as it was told to him by an old man from Camargo: "Villa caught the women in the train at the town and some Chinese too. One of the women, an officer's wife, took a pot shot at Villa while he was killing off the Chinamen. The Chinese, trying to escape, would say: 'Don't shoot me standing; shoot me running.' Then they massacred the women. Three days later, when the Federals came, the babies were still trying to suck at the breasts of the dead women."

Unperturbed, Pancho afterwards rested in the Sierra Madre. He had nothing to do now but watch the rainy season set in and the brilliantly plumaged red and green *guacamayo* birds fight with the blackbirds for shelter in the giant *piños* trees.

General Pershing's Expedition, after an absence of eleven months, returned to Fort Bliss, in El Paso, on February 7, 1917. This officially terminated his remarkable and, until this day, mystifying campaign. He brought back a claim and not his man, for he had routed the gamecock, not killed him. Yet there was truth in the claim he now made of having reduced Villa from a belligerent to a non-combatant. The *hombre* was wounded and almost out of munitions. He had further evidence for his belief that the *banda* was too decimated to reorganize effectively in such enemy casualties as Colonels Julio Cardenas and Candelario Cervantes, as well as such a distinguished enemy prisoner as General Gutierrez. Pershing's campaign certainly added two or three important landmarks to American military annals. For the first time, Americans in combat employed overhead machine guns, rounded up their adversaries in motor passenger cars, and dropped supplies to stranded platoons from airplanes. The United States Army likewise profited greatly from its "training" maneuvers in Mexico. Several of Pershing's men later asserted that they more than once sighted Villa and could have seized him easily. One of them, Mr. Robert MacMurphey, said they did not do so because of the impending conflict in Europe. On April 16, America declared war on Germany.

Anyhow, the great Pancho escaped scot free, endearing himself forever to his countrymen for having outwitted General Pershing. Most of his partisans contended that he should not have been hounded at all. The broadside, *La persecución de Villa,* summarized the whole episode. It first narrated how twelve thousand *gringos* crossed the border to chastize him for a *"desliz,"* his error of invading Columbus. It then told how the Americans repeatedly organized pursuits without coming into contact with him and how they "returned very sad and tired." Texans in particular were reviled, being addressed as "The 'little soldiers' who came all the way from Texas" . . . and as those " 'poor little ones' who wanted to go home."

> All the people there in Ciudad Juárez,
> All were left astonished
> To see so many American soldiers
> Who were hanged on posts by Pancho Villa.

Further on Villa's escape became a kind of victory, and the *corrido* continued.

> What did these Americans think,
> That fighting was a masquerade ball?
> With their faces full of shame
> They returned to their country once more.

Ever the winner and never the loser, the legendary Villa emerged triumphant from the struggle with Pershing. There was no place for defeat in his epic, so that *La persecución* ended in patriotic fervor.

> The *gringos* know that in Mexico they kill,
> And they die daily here.
> While there remains a single Mexican soldier,
> Our flag will fly in his hands.

Full of derring-do as these songs and stories were, one tale of Villa's doings outstripped them all. When Pershing's soldiers were once looking for him, some of Villa's men told them he could be taken at Carrizal; but when they attacked there (June, 1916), they learned that they had been hoodwinked and that the enemy they now engaged were Carranzistas, not Villistas, as expected. At this last major encounter with the Americans, Pancho Villa, before a window safe at his headquarters a slight distance away, saw through his binoculars the entire scene of his two adversaries as they battered out each other's brains. To Mexico he bequeathed his forte of "entertaining" the *gringos,* having developed this "entertainment" into a sport which, in his day, replaced cock fighting as the national pastime.

CHAPTER 12

The Patriot

Ay-yay, Pancho Villa!

After the withdrawal of the Pershing Expeditionary Force, Villa still had to deal with his arch foe, Venustiano Carranza. For a while he rested near Chihuahua, among the hills he loved, thinking hard. The irritating *gringos* had earlier nicked him in the knee cap, but now it had mended and was well. With the *gringos* gone, he had no fears about defeating Carranza. True, his munitions were low, but he knew where he could get money for more. He plotted again, darkly.

Surely Pancho had an unconquerable soul to fight on as he did against the odds. Now the *Dorados* were forever vanished; many of his other prized men had either died or deserted him, and most of his friends were scattered far about the land. The roll of deserters included Generals Chao, Gutierrez, Herrera, and Salazar; the roll of dead, Cardenas, Cervantes, Fierro, Ornelas, Rodríguez, Torbino, and Urbina.

He sensed a touch of winter on the balmiest day when he recollected his old friend Fierro the "Butcherer," who had died at Colonia Dublán or Lake Guzmán. *Ay,* that Fierro was a man after his own heart! The "Butcherer," so a story went, won his sobriquet by slaughtering a multitude of Mexican prisoners in sheer blood lust. He perversely encouraged them to believe that they could win their freedom by running to their prison wall and scaling it. When they came over the top of the wall, Fierro shot each one of them dead. The memory of this old henchman warmed Villa's hard heart.

During 1918, Villa began hanging around his old associate, General Felipe Ángeles, a famous artillery expert. With his aid, Villa every day drew new men to the support of his colors. Before the end of the year, his army swelled from five hundred to two thousand men. Now he spent hour on hour with General Ángeles. That winter they mapped out plans, avidly plotting their course for a major attack in the spring on some strategic city in northern Mexico. He trembled with the old excitement of killing and longed for the sound of cannon fire, for the odor of gunpowder. Much farther back in his consciousness dwelled the idea of emancipating the enslaved masses from their feudal status.

Rightfully figuring its people would assist him, Pancho selected for attack a city which had always worshipped him. He threw his men at Parral on April 25, 1919, and quelled its few, half-hearted defenders. As an avenging deliverer, he strung up the dictatorial mayor and his two sons in the public square, ridding the *peones* of their oppressors. He tried hard but vainly to seize one of his oldest enemies, General Maclovio Herrera. Failing that, he tied nooses about the necks of members of Herrera's family and suspended them from the tops of telephone poles. Villa had gone berserk again, which spelled a bad fate for his foes and not the best one for him, because the blood lust impaired his judgment and his timing. Thus, when he next hurtled his forces at Chihuahua City, he overcame General Jacinto Trevino, but had to relinquish the capital through his neglect to bring up supplies. This mistake showed him that he needed at least another month for reorganization and further planning. Hence, he rested the last days of April and all the month of May.

Early in June, a band of Villistas under Pancho moved towards the Rio Grande and, on the tenth, occupied the northern town of Guadalupe, thirty-two miles southeast of Juárez. That night the Villistas watered their horses well in the river, accepted a few volunteers into their ranks from the disgruntled farmers of Guadalupe, and swigged *tequila* until they fell down prostrate in the streets to drop off to sleep. Of his old band, only his right-hand man, Miguel Trillo, still stayed with him. Most of his new outfit consisted of a different kind of soldier. These new men distinguished themselves, not as fighters, but as drunkards and dope addicts. They drank Guadalupe dry before the dawn. Plagued next morning with hangovers and nervous from the *marihuana,* the new Villistas contrasted sharply with the *Dorados* of old. The night of June 13 they spent in the border village of Zaragosa, a prearranged meeting place for Villa and General Ángeles. During the evening, Villa reviewed the final details for sacking Juárez with Ángeles, who outlined the order of battle and pointed out on a map the advantages of seizing the Juárez race track as early as possible.

On June 15, General Villa, at the head of fifteen hundred men, tried to outface the Carranzistas in Juárez. When they refused to surrender the city, Villa and Ángeles proceeded to take it by force. They demolished their enemies in the space of hours, riding their sweaty horses into the heart of the city, with Villa astride his horse conspicuous in the foreground.

This was the third time in his career that Villa had conquered Juárez. Between that beautiful moonlit June midnight and the fateful red daybreak of June 16 the city rocked to its foundations with revelry. All the pent-up frustrations of the Villistas during past months of inaction found full release in one mad night. Wandering street minstrels joined with the vocal Villistas in singing, over and over again, the four battle hymns of the Revolution: *Adelita, Cucaracha, Marcha Zacatecas,* and *Valentina. Marcha Zacatecas* pleased Villa much; its stirring music set his blood afire and made his black eyes dance with excitement. In every bar, accordions and *concertinas* swelled, subsided, and swelled again with Latin love songs. With voices mellowed by *tequila,* the singers cut loose on Villa's favorite "hymn"—*La Cucaracha:*

> *La cucaracha, la cucaracha.*
> *Ya no puede caminar;*
> *Porque no tiene, porque no tiene,*
> *Marihuana que fumar.*

> The cucaracha, the cucaracha,
> Can no longer walk,
> Because it hasn't, because it hasn't,
> Marihuana to smoke.

Fist fights, at which the Villistas excelled, began and ended over the *putas,* until finally enterprising "promoters" brought in an abundance of girls, moon-bosomed and starry-eyed. The air soured with the stench of *cer-*

veza, cheap perfume, and *los retretes.* Heavy Mexican cigarette smoke thickened into a light blue pall. *Señores y señoritas* continuously staggered up and down the streets, sometimes falling upon the ground in dark alleys, at others toppling through the swinging doors of the *cantinas.* Everybody became drunk with liquor, with fighting, with singing, with love-making. Nobody did any shooting, but sometimes a shining knife blade flashed: the red blood of the victim looked purple against his olive skin. It was the longest, maddest night of the entire Revolution. "Don" Pancho Villa had come home again to Juárez, his city, and long before dawn broke this gamecock crowed until his throat hoarsened and his neck jerked out of place. He and his madcap *mozos* forgot tomorrow. *Mañana?* What mattered a tomorrow after this night that set their wits awhirl?

Next morning few of the Villistas were in a condition to fight, and so the Carranzistas overpowered them with ease. Some of the drunken *hombres* were shot down as they stumbled towards their headquarters at the race track; those already fallen were trampled underfoot by Federal horsemen. Others made it to the race track and swarmed about their beaten leader, "Señor" Pancho Villa.

Could he now, after such an orgy, pass another miracle and reorganize his rabble?

He could not. There was too much of the past stacked against him. Hereafter the present would remain for him a day-by-day proposition; never was the future to put him back in the saddle again. His fighting days were done with.

As Villa stood ruminating at the race track, the United States Army swept to the aid of Carranza. Several United States cavalry troops galloped across the Rio Grande, with two thousand American Negro soldiers marching in their wake. A realization of his utter ruin, like a shaft of frozen steel, pierced Villa's heart. Hurriedly he deserted the battlefield.

His partner, General Felipe Ángeles, moved onward to attack Villa Ahumada after leaving Juárez, but Villa stayed out of the battle. Ángeles next went on without Villa to attack Chihuahua City, to be captured, and to be executed. A *corrido* included the horrible details of his demise:

> With his intestines protruding outside
> And in convulsions of agony,
> He received the *coup de grace*
> Which brought an end to his days.

Lucky Pancho Villa, who remained behind! At the close of 1919 he knew when enough was enough.

In 1920, General Obregon joined Generals Calles and Adolfo de la Huerta in a plot to kill Carranza on May 21. This new triumvirate of Obregon, Calles, and de la Huerta looked formidable to Villa. Besides, he remembered all too well Calles at Agua Prieta and that chimera, the Sonoran campaign. In rapid succession President de la Huerta succeeded Carranza, and then President Obregon succeeded de la Huerta. For a moment Villa dreamed of migrating to South America. Then the influential author, Elias Torres, came to his aid. Señor Torres said that he would intercede with the Federal authorities in the general's behalf and secure for him honorable retirement. Villa stood at the end of a long trail, having traveled from pillage to peace.

Seeking the role of hero to the last, Villa surrendered himself on the grounds that he wanted to avoid a war between Mexico and the United States. As he disappeared behind the curtain from the spotlight of international interest, he created the impression of a *gran hombre* able to take his medicine through love of country. The terms of his retirement were munificent: he retained his rank of general with full pay, and received, as a reward for his past services, ownership of the important *El Rancho del Canutillo*. Hereafter he would live a tranquil life, as ordered and predictable as the usual flow of the Rio Grande. But before he retired to his ranch near Parral, he took care of his future and, in the epic style, made a successful bid for lasting fame. The mediators had, at last, dissuaded him from murder and massacre. In saying farewell to his friend Elias Torres, he asked him to do something for him, to tell the people he was never beaten. *"Dile a la gente que Pancho Villa nunca se rindio,"* he said. With these parting words he launched the proud myth of his invincibility.

CHAPTER 13

The Pumpkin-seed Vendor

In the environs of the rock-fenced city of Parral, at his stupendous ranch of 25,000 acres, General Francisco Villa, "Retired," lived in supreme magnificence. He enjoyed, in the year 1920, the first peace he had experienced since his earliest childhood days at *hacienda* Rio Grande. He had cause to be serene: he had a celebrated name, a good wife, fine children, and money saved away in the bank and jingling in his pockets. After a career of turbulence unmatched in the twentieth century, he now owned his *rancho grande,* which was given to him by his grateful country as a reward for his military services. He now busied himself with farming in a welcome respite from storm and battle. He employed his *peones* in the constructive work of modernizing Parral as well as his own splendiferous new estate—*El Rancho de Canutillo.*

Pancho had a knack for organization, as shown when he had built Juárez into an efficient city. He also had the proverbial gold thumb, so that little time passed before he owned a bank in Parral. With profits from the bank, the 500,000 gold *pesos* which his government paid him as a retired general, and the hoardings of a lifetime, he straightway installed all available new improvements on his *rancho.* He bought tractors, combines, motors, and various types of modern farm machinery from the United States; he placed his economy on a sound, business-like basis. He built rock fences about his land and led other farmers to do likewise. Instead of lolling in the sun and letting the land do as it wished about supporting him, he listened to Americans acquainted with scientific methods of agriculture and worked with the aim in mind of making Canutillo a paying investment. In the first year he spent thousands of dollars in putting the land and machinery in fine condition, but the gain from his first crops proved sufficient to show him that he had a profitable enterprise on his hands.

A strong factor in his success as a *ranchero* was his knowledge of men. He made them walk the chalkline and give up *tequila* and women. He instructed them to stay with their wives and children and to stop philandering with the "girls" in town. He rounded his *peones* into a community, encouraged "country socials" of singing and dancing. He helped them, but he forced them to labor for their earnings, encouraging them to have a sense of integrity and self-respect. Perhaps he eased their lot because he had himself suffered so much as a *peon muchacho* on the *rancho* owned by the López Negretes. Yet, at the same time, he enforced rules of behavior and self-discipline with the rigidity of an old army man. When men had to be punished, he or one of his associates horsewhipped them publicly as an object lesson. Then he forgave them and sent them back to the fields. Talking softly but firmly, he developed his voice at this time into a cat-like purr befitting a rich *grandee*. He epitomized the benevolent despot.

Maybe he nurtured the idea that later on he could teach other farmers to follow his example, that he could peacefully renovate the feudal system of Mexico by an agrarian revolution. Sweat and work might succeed where sword and fire had failed. Nobody knew what dreams he now fostered. The full portrait of the retired Villa should comprise his new virtues, not only his old vices. For now the number of merits to be cited in his behalf grew daily. Maybe the *peones* were right, people began to reason, in their high estimate of him.

To prosper his schemes, Villa entertained notables and influential business men and made them his friends. Throughout his career he had managed to be on good terms with great Americans. In his military days along the Great River of the North, he had cultivated and entertained General Pershing, with whom he went hunting. He also knew General Scott, who proved a loyal friend to the last. At some time in his early career, he encountered the famous American writer, Ambrose Bierce, and delved into the character of this temperamental, hard-drinking literary genius who later disappeared mysteriously into Mexico, to die of old age, privations, or at the hands of a thoughtless killer. Now he met the American business man and adventurer, Jimmie Caldwell, from whom he bought thousands of dollars of farm machinery. Mr. Caldwell also served as his foreman, giving him invaluable advice about the operation of the new machinery and about the cultivating and rotating of crops. The distinguished American writer, Frazier Hunt, visited *El Rancho de Canutillo* and formed a favorable opinion of Villa. Throughout the period of the Revolution he knew well Mr. Harris Walthall, United States collector of customs for the twenty-fourth district, who said: "I think he was perfectly sincere in wanting to do something for the *peones* of Mexico both during and after the Revolution." He corresponded with many notables whom he did not meet in person. He ordered his stationery from England, with his name embossed thereon in dignified lettering. His secretary, Miguel Trillo, took care of the correspondence. He appended to each letter his flourishing signature "Francisco Villa," for he preferred suitable formality and never stooped to using the familiar form of "Pancho" in his epistles. At Canutillo, General Villa went a long way toward re-establishing himself in civilized society.

Once people began talking about the new Villa, they tended to remember his good deeds of earlier days. He was not, they said, such a bad sort after all. Did they not recall how he had befriended a young man called Pablito, a motorcycle rider, who died in the second battle of Parral and whose mother the General had then sent a huge sum of money? Did they not recall how he had given a blind old codger named Don Tomás a thousand *pesos* so he would not lose his ranch? Assuredly, everybody must have remembered how he had fed the starving town of Villa Ahumada, had ordered four merchants and the owner of the flour mill to do his bidding, and had made it a death penalty for storekeepers to conceal or hoard food. Assuredly they recalled the episode of the musician. He met young Rafael Mendez, now a noted musician in Hollywood, during the Revolution. When Mendez said he wanted to play for General Obregon, he told him: "I ought to shoot you, but a good trumpet player should never die. I'll send you home instead." And the *gran hombre* did, with a cavalry escort, but only after the musician had played Villa's favorite *Marcha Zacatecas* again and again.

Throughout the year 1922, Villa's star shone with considerable brilliance. Respectable citizens toasted him as a fine family man, as a thoughtful father. In December, he sent his two young sons, Agustino (ten) and Octavio (twelve) to school in Texas, where they shopped in El Paso before going on to their destination, a private school in San Antonio. Yes, the General was a generous man. Had he not taken care of the poor of Parral? In two central stanzas of the *corrido La rendición* he emerged as a support to the weak:

> He has a great heart,
> That famous *guerrillero,*
> And all the North loves him
> And looks after him with care.

> He has protected the poor
> And also the aged,
> And those who ask him for help
> Never depart without it.

In those days the course of his life ran so smoothly that he almost forgot his tempestuous past.

Then the lull ended. A band of cattle rustlers stole over a hundred head of his cattle. Worse yet, three men crept up unseen in the fields and tried to kill him while he was loading hay. Their motive? *Quien sabe?* An Eastern company in the United States refused to insure either Villa or Miguel Trillo, regarding them both as too great a risk. He was not so secure, after all, and trembled a little at the change in his fortune.

By the beginning of 1923, dark clouds clustered about the General's bright star. He still sought to override the mounting criticism. To prove his fair intentions, he re-conditioned the road between *El Rancho de Canutillo* and Parral. He spent money right and left. He poured two million *pesos* into his own ranch, into equipment and buildings. His old magnetic charm began to reassert itself. He bought people drinks and hired anybody and everybody to work for him. He purred to the matrons, stroking his fine mustache, which now no longer drooped but curled sharply upward. The married ladies were, he assured them, his *mangos de Manila*. He tried smiling at everybody, especially all the good-looking *señoras*. Could it be that sometimes he smiled at the wrong parties?

There were oldsters alive who feared revival of the Rebellion. Too many *corridos* reminded them of his gory past.

> Hurrah for Villa, boys!
> Fix the machine guns.
>
> Listen, Francisco Villa,
> What does your heart tell you?
>
> Don't you remember, brave one,
> That you attacked Paredón;
> Don't you remember, brave one,
> That you took Torreón?

Too many foul atrocities blackened his name. Only yesterday massacres had occurred everywhere. No sane citizen of Parral wanted a return of those good old days!

Then conditions improved, but only momentarily. His oldest enemy, General Maclovio Herrera, died of old age. He had hated him with a passion. Once again General Villa allowed a smile to come slowly over his face. The blood on his pudgy hands was dyed too deep, however, to be washed away in one or two cleansings. He could not reach into the past to unwind the clocks of time. The Spaniards in Mexico rankled at the mention of his name and cursed him with mouth-filling oaths, damning his "black soul" to everlasting purgatory. Far too many of these patricians, the Terrazas and the Herreras, had been ruined by him. To the *peones* alone, who were blinded by their adoration, he remained a benefactor. He did his utmost to purr softly. Still he smiled —or tried to.

The more he smiled the more the gossip circulated. They said he had killed too many men. One rumor was particularly grisly—and persistent. A lot of men talked about being afraid for their wives. They said that Villa, aged forty-five, had regained splendid new vigor from farm life. The rumor was impossible to deny, he strutted about so continuously, like a rooster crowing his clarion of *qui-qui-ri-quí.*

And then one day—Friday, July 20, 1923—General Villa, homeward bound, drove his Dodge automobile out of Parral. Miguel Trillo, faithful unto the end, sat upright beside him in front and Rosalio Morales, with two bodyguards, in back. A conspiratorial pumpkin-seed vendor, standing beside a tree, suddenly shouted *"Viva Villa!"* The general slowed his car, lifting a hand to salute the *peon.* Immediately a fusillade of shots rang out. All the occupants of the car, except a bodyguard who escaped never again to reappear, slumped over dead. Sixteen bullets lodged in the big body of Villa, four in his unrepentant head.

From that time forward, no two eye-witnesses ever agreed on what happened. Where did the assassination occur? Some said in the street directly opposite the Hidalgo Hotel owned by Villa himself. Others said near the Guanajato Bridge. Why was he murdered? Some declared that he played too freely with other men's womenfolk. Others said that he planned to start a new revolution. Still others claimed he was killed by friends of his old enemy, Herrera. Who shot him? Some said General Calles and Gabriel Chavez, General Motors car dealer, engineered the whole plot. Others named Congressman Jesus Salas Barrazas, of the El Oro district of Durango, who had long kept a spy on Villa's ranch and who once, long ago, had been pistol-whipped by Villa in an argument over a woman. On the day of the assassination the Federal police arrested nobody. Later they traced Barrazas to Jiménez and placed him in custody. The courts sentenced him to twenty years, but he served only six months.

Shortly before his death, in Mexico City, in 1951, Barrazas made a full statement. He did not regret having killed Villa and declared that he would do the same again if Villa were to come to life *("si resucitara lo volveria a matar")*. He denied María Luz Corral de Villa's claim that the assassination was plotted by General Calles and Chavez, the car dealer. He said the murder occurred on July 11, not July 20, and was committed by seven persons: Meliton Lozoya, Juan José Saiz and his cousin José Saiz Prado Prado, two of the Guerra brothers, Ruperto Vera, and Salas Barrazas. In his statement Barrazas said at the end: "I'm not a murderer. I rid humanity of a monster."

Even after his death, the body of Villa was denied a peaceful resting place. The people buried General Villa at Parral. Three years later, in 1926, the American adventurer Captain Emil L. Holmdahl was arrested in Parral on the charge of opening the tomb and removing the head. The officials charged that he took it to sell to American scientists. Holmdahl calmly denied the charge. Friends of Emil Holmdahl, in El Paso, wired American officials at Parral to intercede in his behalf and they arranged his release. When Holmdahl later appeared in El Paso at the Sheldon Hotel, it is claimed that he had the head with him and displayed it to close friends in the privacy of his room. The tale seems highly unlikely. But this, though many years intervened, was not the last to be heard of Holmdahl. In 1952, he was questioned in Los Angeles by Secret Service agents seeking a mysterious hoard of twenty millions of gold ingots buried somewhere in the Southwest. Had he stolen Villa's gold from the Sierra Madre? Since Holmdahl was notoriously adventurous, it would be hard to put it past him. The ballad *La decapitación* stated that he stole Villa's head for money:

> Such a strange infamy
> Would never have been conceived
> If gold had not been valued
> Higher than manly honor.

In 1950, María Luz Corral de Villa ordered her husband's body removed from the cemetery in Parral to a mausoleum he earlier had built in the Panteon de la Regla, in Chihuahua City, but one of his other widows and his two sons, Doctor Francisco Villa and Attorney Hipolito Villa, joined together to prevent the removal. No further chance has ever presented itself for examining the remains to see if the head is still attached.

Why have the remains of Villa undergone such tribulations? This, the *peones* say, must always be the fate of an impious man. They assert that his spirit has suffered in the other world because he disrespected the clergy. He executed Father Dionico Triana on a shaky charge of treason. Was he justified in forcing Luisa Garcia, a pregnant girl of fifteen, to marry a priest, Señor Cura? They forgot that he did this because she had falsely accused him at the guilty priest's insistence. Others said that sometimes his attitude toward the clergy bordered on sacrilege. One time he had commanded his men to fire upon the church steeple at Santa Rosalia. The men were barely prevented from doing so by the appearance of the Virgin herself. Yet again he once encountered a wealthy Juárez minister and objected to the way he wore his expensive collar. When the minister fearfully explained that he was no intruder but a citizen of Mexico, Pancho let him go.

Oddly enough, the Mexicans blamed the *gringos,* not Barrazas, for Pancho's death. The *corrido La decapitación* maintained that

> The Yankees were not able
> To defeat him in a fair fight,
> So they cut off his head
> Since he cannot hold them to account.

Mournfully, another broadside, *La muerte,* addressed the *paloma:*

Fly, fly, little dove;
Light on that small fig tree,
And tell all the *gringos*
That Pancho Villa is dead.

The irony of Villa's assassination was not that he
lived by a gun and died by a gun. A vicious scorpion
lives in Mexico called the *alacrán,* which gives birth to
but one litter of baby scorpions. It gives birth but once
because the little scorpions remain attached to their par-
ent and devour its body. The irony of Pancho Villa's
death is that he, like a human *alacrán,* uplifted and nurtured the lowly caste, one of whom, a mere pumpkin-
seed vendor, betrayed him to his bloodthirsty assassins.

CHAPTER 14

Ghost of the Rio Grande

The *peones* of Juárez will long remember their man Villa. *Ay, ay, Pancho*—there was the *grand hombre* for you! He was afraid of nobody, that Pancho; not of the Mexican *gobernadores* nor the *gringos* of the United States. He was their one true friend and made his rallying cry, *"Maten los ricos!"*

The *peones*, were they right or wrong about their hero? In their minds, Pancho had to be accepted as a fact of nature. He was as much a part of their life and of their dreams as any other natural phenomenon—as the Rio Grande itself. Nobody on this earth could stop the murderous rage of their Pancho once his firecracker temper ignited. Only an *hombre* gone *loco* would blame Pancho for his impetuosity; their leader simply did things in a natural, spontaneous way. All one needed to do was to wait. He loved the people. His spirit would yet inspire a successful revolution. Underneath his angry demeanor the heart of a true friend of the people pumped rich, hot blood.

The *peones* knew he was the ferocious *hombre* who could ride a hundred nights without resting, take a hundred women in succession, and kill a hundred *rurales* by himself in a gun fight. When all the *politicos* veered from one party to another, he stood like an immovable bulwark above their petty squabbling in his unceasing defense of the suffering masses. When Francisco Indalecio Madero lay dead in his coffin, he swore through the black mustache drooping over his adenoidal mouth to keep alive the ideals of the Revolution. Call him "bloody murderer," as the Spaniards did, yet he cared for the lowly. Call him a sadistic killer of helpless Americans, as the *gringos* did, yet he may have paid the New Mexican merchant at Columbus for ammunition never delivered to him. Call him a defiler of women, as the clergy did, yet a hard-working housemaid or two later testified in El Paso how Villa freed them from the brothels to labor honestly and live in cleanliness beneath the healing sun.

To the *peones,* the incomparable Villa was truly a *gran bandido,* that and much more besides. They talk about his vengeful spirit as well as about how he always feared for his life. Nowadays on the border, youngsters spin tales of him, depicting him as the toughly heroic. Felipa Zavala, an El Paso schoolgirl, tells an incident about him: "Pancho Villa went to a restaurant. He asked for some lunch. Pancho Villa started eating his lunch. He found that the food they served him had poison. Then Pancho Villa killed everybody that was in the restaurant. He killed the ones that were eating their own lunch just because he found out his lunch had poison." Children have a nature myth about him, too. In stormy weather they ask their mothers who it is that thunders in the heavens. The mothers say, "That is Pancho Villa!" The peasants have envisaged him as a rich man, a heavy eater who got "fat in the kidneys."

This picture has comforted them in their own penury, because each of them, at one time or another, has dreamed of finding Villa's hidden loot or one of his lost mines. Some of them believe that he returns as a ghost.

The ghost who haunts the Rio Grande is *muy rico*. Mrs. Manuel D. Hornedo, of El Paso, heard a story about his gold from her washerwoman. She claimed that once, while visiting her brother Jesus in Juárez, they used to see a spirit haunting a *tapia,* or mud wall, behind her brother's house. She thought that treasure might be buried there and wanted him to help her dig for it. He objected at first but then was persuaded to do so. They found a hole, but it contained bricks, not gold. Soon afterwards, however, a woodcutter named José Tovar saw a ghost at Palo Chino, near Juárez.

"*Oyes, José,*" the ghost said, "you were with me in the *revolución.*"

"I was with you?"

"*Sí, compadre,* can it be that you do not remember."

"*Pues, sí,*" José said, "I was in the *revolución,* but who are you?"

"I am Pancho Villa."

"No, I do not believe it. I can't see your face; it is all shadowy."

"Yes, *amigo,* I am Pancho Villa and I am suffering."

The ghost told José that the gold was in some leather sacks beneath a mound of painted rocks close by. José became too frightened to look for the treasure and ran home to his wife. For about two weeks he remained deathly sick, until finally nightly prayers brought him back to sound health. He never saw the ghost again.

More recently, *peones* have seen at night eerie camp-

fires burning near the Rio Grande on the old race track
southeast of Juárez. Policemen have gone to investigate
the fires but have found nothing. The campfires always
are seen at precisely the spot where Villa and his *Dorados* were accustomed to encamp.

On rare occasions the ghost is said to appear without
its head. The reason why Villa's headless *bulto* continues
to walk about at night is that he wants to locate his skull
and so be able to rest in peace. The ghost is greatly dis-
turbed by the loss of his *cabeza,* for before he died he
had the map of his great treasure in the Sierra Madre
tattooed on the top of his scalp and covered by the long
front locks of his hair. He remains troubled through
fear that his skull will be found by a despicable *gringo*.
The *bulto* desires either to keep the treasure for himself
or to give it to a *peon*. The trouble is that sight of the
wraith has thus far frightened the *peones* whom he
wants to help.

Such stories explain why the ghost of Pancho Villa
today roams Juárez, on the brown banks of the Rio
Grande. Sometimes he is seen talking with another shadowy spirit, that of old Ignacio Parra, his bandit friend
of yore. At times, he materializes in the south, walking
the country lanes of Parral. He comes by midnight to
lift a lowly *peon* and urge him to rise above his servi-
tude. And there is cause for these tales. What of his head,
which was severed from his body? How much of him
remains in the Parral grave? Why is the splendid mausoleum at Chihuahua City an empty tomb?

In the *corrido, La muerte,* the symbol of Villa the
unconquerable persists, so that the past does not contain
him fully:

Though you may not like it, I repeat
In these plain and honest words
That young roosters like Pancho Villa
Are not born every day.

Qui-qui-ri-quí! Qui-qui-ri-quí!
As long as tales are told in Mexico, Pancho Villa will
live on.

Sources

The source materials of this saga come in part from books, magazines, and newspapers but principally from numerous informants. The descriptive passages are not imaginary, but based on travel sketches and my own observation of Mexican scenery.

1. Articles and Books

Arnold, Oren: "We Remember Pancho," *Thunder in the Southwest,* Norman, Oklahoma, 1952 (anecdotes about his cruelty and daring).

Azuela, Mariano: *Los de Abajo,* ed. John E. Englekirk and Lawrence B. Kiddle, New York, 1939 (a celebrated novel about Villa and his times).

Braddy, Haldeen: "Pancho Villa, Man and Hero," *Southwest Review* (1937), XXII, 338-342 (tales about his cruelty as well as his heroism).

————— "Pancho Villa, Folk Hero of the Mexican Border," *Western Folklore* (1948), VII, 349-355 (tales about him as a hero of the people).

————— "Dorotello Arango, *alias* Pancho Villa," *New Mexico Folklore Record* (1950), V, 4-8 (Villa's birth and early beginnings).

————— "Man of a Million Faces," *Texas Parade* (1952), XII, 26-27 (he was a human enigma).

————— "The Faces of Pancho Villa," *Western Folklore* (1952), XI, 93-99 (his roles in history and legend).

————— "Pancho Villa's Hidden Loot," *Western Folklore* (1953), XII, 77-84 (tales of his buried treasures).

————— and McNeely, John H.: "Francisco Villa in Folk-Songs," *Arizona Quarterly* (1954), X, 5-16 (*corridos* about Villa and his men).

Bush, Dr. I. J.: *The Gringo Doctor,* Caldwell, Idaho, 1939 (personal reminiscences of life on the border).

Campobello, Nellie: *Apuntes sobre la vida militar de Francisco Villa,* Mexico, D. F., 1940 (Villa acclaimed a great strategist; also his confession about hiding gold is narrated).

Dromundo, Balthasar: *Villa y Adelita,* Durango, 1936 (a love story together with the text of the song *Adelita*).

Foix, Pere: *Pancho Villa,* Mexico, D. F., 1950 (his whole life story).

Gilpatric, Guy: *Flying Stories,* New York, 1946 (facts about Villa's fliers in the Introduction).

González, Manuel W.: *Contra Villa,* Mexico, D. F., 1935 (the record for and against Villa).

Guzmán, Martin Luis: *El Aguilar y la Serpiente,* Mexico, D. F., 1941 (a novel of the Revolution now regarded as a classic).

Hague, Eleanor: *Spanish American Folk-Songs,* New York, 1917 (especially *"Boanerges," "En los montes más remotos,"* and *"No hay árbol"*).

Harris, Larry: *Pancho Villa and the Columbus Raid,* El Paso, 1949 (based in good measure on newspaper accounts).

Horgan, Paul: *Great River,* New York, 1954, 2 vols. (volume two includes a factual report of the Columbus raid and of Villa's rampages along the Rio Grande).

Lea, Tom: "The Affair of the Fifteen Aprils," *Southwest Review* (1951), XXXVI, 8-12 (the episode of Villa and a fornicating priest translated into English from the book by Torres).

Marcosson, Isaac F.: *Metal Magic, The Story of the American Smelting and Refining Company,* New York, 1949 (anecdotes about Villa and the miners).

Navarro, Esteban A.: *The Ills of Mexico by a Mexican,* Chicago, 1914 (a contemporary statement by a fiery patriot).

Niggli, Josephina: "Soldadera," *The Best One-Act Plays of 1937,* ed. Margaret Mayorga, New York, 1938 (a dramatized story of the Villistas, their liquor, *marihuana,* and women).

Parker, Dr. George: *Guaracha Trail,* New York, 1951 (an autobiography with reminiscences about the Villistas).

Reid, Raymond J.: *The Mormons in Chihuahua,* University of New Mexico M. A. Thesis, Albuquerque, 1938 (contains valuable primary evidence on Villa and the Mormons).

Sandburg, Carl: "Memoir of a Proud Boy," *Cornhuskers,* New York, 1918 (Don Magregor and Villa).

Schuster, Dr. Otto: *Pancho Villa's Shadow,* New York, 1947 (an intimate close-up of Villa by a man who knew him).

Scott, General Hugh L.: *Some Memories of a Soldier,* New York, 1928 (reminiscences here and there of his association and dealings with Villa).

Stevens, Louis: *Here Comes Pancho Villa,* New York, 1930 (emphasizes Villa's villainy in a racy story of him and his cruel men).

Tompkins, Col. Frank: *Chasing Villa,* Harrisburg, Pa., 1934 (the fullest factual account but too detailed for easy perusal).

Toor, Frances: *A Treasury of Mexican Folkways,* New York, 1947 (especially a few tales about Villa and the other world).

Torres, Elias L.: *Vida y Hazañas de Pancho Villa,* Mexico, D. F., 1921 (an authoritative statement by Villa's friend).

Toulmin, Harry Aubrey: *With Pershing in Mexico,* Harrisburg, Pa., 1935 (an engrossing book; excellent description of the terrain, Columbus raid, aftermath).

Turner, Timothy G.: *Bullets, Bottles, and Gardenias,* Dallas, 1935 (includes anecdotes about the battle of Agua Prieta).

Villa, Luz Corral vda. de: *Pancho Villa en la Intimidad,* Mexico, D. F., 1948 (a spirited defense and biographical recital by Villa's wife).

White, Owen P.: *Out of the Desert,* El Paso, 1924 (Villa's career in the border country, especially his battles for Juárez).

2. Magazines and Newspapers

Albuquerque Tribune:
    On the Columbus raid and Jesus Paiz (March 8, 1950).
Chicago Tribune:
    On reports of the Columbus raid by Arthur Ravel and Lee Riggs (June 13, 1919).
El Fronterizo (Juárez):
    On Barrazas and his assassination of Villa (January 7, 1951).
El Paso Herald:
    Governor Gonzales of Chihuahua made his last will and testament in El Paso (November 22, 1910).
    On J. S. Alvarez's purchase of ammunition in El Paso for Villa (December 8, 1910).
    On the outbreak of the Mexican insurrection and the siege of Ojinaga (December 16, 1910).
El Paso Herald Post:
    On Emil Holmdahl and Villa's head (February 9, 1926).
    On Villa's friend Tracy Richardson (April 23, 1949).

On Villa's mausoleum in Chihuahua (May 10, 1950).

On Villa's censoring the news from Mexico (June 18, 1953).

El Paso Times:

On the Columbus raid (December 3, 10, 1950).

On El Paso nurses and Villa's wounded (January 7, 1951).

On Villa's buried treasure on Mount Franklin (April 15, 1951).

On Villa's Dodge automobile (January 31, 1952).

On the New Mexico University students and Villa's gold (January 31, 1952).

On Emil Holmdahl and the twenty millions of gold ingots (Sept. 29, 1952).

On soldiers of fortune with Villa (March 22, 1953).

On the first battle of Juárez (May 17, 1953).

On A. R. Carson, Pershing's guide (June 12, 1953).

Hispano americano:

On a photograph of Villa weeping at Madero's tomb (August 25, 1950).

New Mexico (University) Lobo:

On Mrs. Villa's denial that Pancho left a buried treasure (February 7, 1952).

San Antonio Express Magazine:

On Madero's declaration of war against Díaz (November 26, 1950).

Santa Fe New Mexican:

On Mrs. Villa's visit to New Mexico (July 10, 1949).

Time:

On Royce G. Martin and his escape with Mrs. Villa to Cuba (March 16, 1953).

On the roles of Barrazas, Chávez, and the pumpkin-seed vendor in the assassination of Villa (June 4, 1951).

3. Informants

Andrews, R. L. of El Paso, who was an aviator for the Mexican government opposing Villa.

Bosworth, Laniel, of El Paso, who told me a story about the murder of William S. Benton.

Breen, Jack, of Columbus, New Mexico, who related to me anecdotes about Villa's raid on Columbus.

Candelaria, Mr. and Mrs. Fred, of El Paso, who did research on Villa's sojourn in El Paso.

Cooper, Clarence, formerly of Durango and now of El Paso, who told me stories of Villa's deeds in Chihuahua.

Cordova, Gabriel, Jr., of El Paso, who told me a tale about Villa's ghost.

Davis, E. A., of Baton Rouge, Louisiana, who, in Mexico City did research on Villa and his daughter from Durango, Natalia de Paredes.

De La Rue, Mrs. Robert, of Santa Fe, who investigated the Ford-McCormick trial in Michigan and who sent me information about Villa and the musician, Rafael Mendez.

Del Valle, David, of El Paso, who gave me tales of Villa's lost treasure.

Dolan, R. M., of El Paso, who knew Villa personally.

Ehmann, Mr. and Mrs. F. A., of El Paso, who gave me a story about Villa's raid on the Lovrett ranch.

Esquerra, Mrs. Graciela, of Saltillo, Coahuila, who sent me a story about Villa's being the son of a Spanish nobleman.

Fife, Austin, of Los Angeles, who sent me valuable material on Villa and the Mormons.

French, A. L., of Elida, New Mexico, who sent me information about the Columbus raid.

Hill, Fred, of El Paso, who recalled stories of Villa's rustling cattle from his grandfather along the border.

Horncdo, Mrs. Manuel, of El Paso, who told the washerwoman's story of seeing Villa's ghost to Dr. C. L. Sonnichsen, my informant.

House, Mrs. Berta, of El Paso, who narrated the story of Señor Franco and his blind son.

Hunt, Frazier, of Newtown, Bucks County, Pa., who told me of his visit to El Rancho del Canutillo after Villa's death.

Jones, Duncan, of El Paso, who told me about his experiences in Chihuahua and Durango with the Villistas.

Loudon, Nancie, of El Paso, who brought me a number of folktales about Villa's cruelty to women.

Marquez, Alfred, of El Paso, who talked with me about Villa and the mining companies.

Martinez, Mrs. Sadie, of Benson, Arizona, who told me incidents of Villa's Sonoran campaign.

Merari, Mr. and Mrs. C. B., of El Paso, who gave me information about Villa's assassination and the later history of the Dodge automobile in which he was killed.

Navarrez, Rafael, a schoolboy of El Paso, who remembered a tale handed to him about Villa's seeing the Virgin at Camargo.

Navarro, Caterino, of El Paso and Juárez, who indefatigably gathered stories about Villa from old residents along the border.

Norte, Andres, a schoolboy of El Paso, who retold tales he had heard about Villa's running off with pretty women.

Patton, Mrs. Viola Anderson, of El Paso, who retold me tales she had gathered along the border.

Plumb, Edward, of El Paso, who told me stories of his experience as a miner in Chihuahua and also the account of the kidnapping of Frank Knotts.

Reid, Adrian, of El Paso, who gave me the tale of Pablo and Rita Avila, who were murdered in Juárez.

Reuter, Dr. E. G., of San Antonio, who furnished details about Madero's sojourn in San Antonio.

Stebbins, Linda Lee, of Albuquerque, who gave me details about Villa and the Mormons.

Steward, A. M., of Albuquerque, who told me a story about Villa's father being a Mexican general.

Terrazas, Margarita, of El Paso, who told me of Villa's love affairs, his murder of Emiliano E. Terrazas, and his raids on Don Luis.

Torrance, Mrs. R. F., of Naco, Arizona, who told me many anecdotes about Villa in Arizona and Sonora.

Walthall, Harris, of El Paso, who knew Villa for many years along the border.

Ybarra, Lt. Col. Julio Manzano, of Juárez, an old Villista who described to me many important highlights of Pancho's entire career.

Zavala, Felipa, a schoolgirl of El Paso, who retold tales from her grandparents about Villa's fear of having his food poisoned.